Curses and Jinxes

AF801736

Vikas Khatri

PUSTAK MAHAL®
Delhi • Bangalore • Mumbai • Patna • Hyderabad • London

Publishers
Pustak Mahal®, Delhi

J-3/16 , Daryaganj, New Delhi-110002
☎ 23276539, 23272783, 23272784 • *Fax:* 011-23260518
E-mail: info@pustakmahal.com • *Website:* www.pustakmahal.com

London Office
5, Roddell Court, Bath Road, Slough SL3 OQJ, England
E-mail: pustakmahaluk@pustakmahal.com

Sales Centre
10-B, Netaji Subhash Marg, Daryaganj, New Delhi-110002
☎ 23268292, 23268293, 23279900 • *Fax:* 011-23280567
E-mail: rapidexdelhi@indiatimes.com

Branch Offices
Bangalore: ☎ 22234025
E-mail: pmblr@sancharnet.in • pustak@sancharnet.in
Mumbai: ☎ 22010941
E-mail: rapidex@bom5.vsnl.net.in
Patna: ☎ 3294193 • *Telefax:* 0612-2302719
E-mail: rapidexptn@rediffmail.com
Hyderabad: *Telefax:* 040-24737290
E-mail: pustakmahalhyd@yahoo.co.in

© Pustak Mahal, Delhi

ISBN 978-81-223-0971-3

Edition : 2007

The Copyright of this book, as well as all matter contained herein (including illustrations) rests with the Publishers. No person shall copy the name of the book, its title design, matter and illustrations in any form and in any language, totally or partially or in any distorted form. Anybody doing so shall face legal action and will be responsible for damages.

Printed at : Unique Colour Carton, Mayapuri, Delhi-110064

Preface

Curses are Magic spells which are placed upon people with the intention of harming them. The misfortune intended by curses can range from illness, and harm, to even death. Curses are declared to be the most dreaded form of magic, often called black magic, and are believed to be universally used. The principle purposes for them to be "laid" or "thrown" are for revenge, and also for protection of homes, treasures and grave sites. Curses can become effective immediately or may be dormant for years. Curses laid on families have been known to have plagued them for generations.

Sandford Cohen, a psychologist at Boston University, USA, is convinced from field research that curses be can lethal because of the feeling of utter helplessness they can inspire. He sees a striking similarity between a man nowadays dying from fear of some disease generally believed to be fatal, and primitive man dying from a witch doctor's curse.

Another explanation involves the 'tape recording' theory – that a thought can imprint itself on an object or person, and can be transferred to others. If the thought is malevolent, so is the effect. There do seem to be numerous cases of curse victims being totally sceptical of supernatural 'mumbo-jumbo', which nevertheless does nothing to save them from the effects.

Allied to curses are the phenomena known as jinxes, objects that bring bad luck to the owner. This negative belief is contrary to the belief in the mascots – things that are credited with good luck. There are jinxed ships, cars and some statues.

What could be the plausible reason for these curses and jinxes? Is there anything supernatural about them or is it merely a product of fear and tension resulting from the knowledge of the jinxed objects' past. Such psychological origins of curses and jinxes can be accepted as a possibility. The possibility is that either the tragic events themselves create a negative thought field or the fear and nervous tension of the people involved create it, or both. That is, the phenomenon is the product of some sort of interaction between negative thought fields and the people who react to it negatively, either consciously or unconsciously. Perhaps curses and jinxes can be beaten back by strong forces of positive thoughts and a humanist approach to life in general and to specific objects in particular. But this, in any case, is only a hypothesis.

Contents

1. Catching the Souls of the Dead

The most terrifying of all apparitions are those which come to call people to their graves. Once such a spirit is seen, death is inevitable. These fearful beings are found in all parts of the world. Though they take many guises and shapes, their purpose as harbingers of death is never in doubt.

Possibly the most dramatic and noisiest of these terrible beings are the banshees. Each banshee attaches itself to a particular family. Such families are usually the old noble Gaelic families of Ireland. When a member of the family is due to die, the banshee pays a visit.

The coming of the banshee is always a frightening and weird experience. The first manifestation of the banshee is usually a low moaning cry or a gentle sobbing. After several minutes this sound rises in volume and pitch to become a hideous scream of despair. The terrible sound then fades away to gentle sobbing. Sometimes the banshee will wail and cry for several days before death claims its victims. On other occasions only a single, horrific cry will be heard.

The banshee who utters the call is not seen as often as she is heard. But the few people who have gazed upon the banshee describe her as a beautiful young woman dressed in a long green dress and grey shawl.

Perhaps the most famous man whose death was foretold by a banshee was King Brian Boru who died as he fought an army of Vikings in 1014.

But it is not only noble families who are visited by the banshee, nor is the spirit confined to Ireland. Banshees seem able to follow the family which they haunt across the world. Many less distinguished people are descended from ancient families. It can sometimes be surprising where the banshee wails.

James O'Barry, an American businessman of Irish descent, has heard the banshee wail twice, when his grandfather and father died. In 1979, a terrible wailing split the air at Winchester, England. A member of the McCormack family died almost at once. The banshee has even been seen in the middle of a battlefield. During the First World War, a young man named Daniel O'Conner was serving in the British army in France. In 1915, the regiment was ordered forwards to attack a German position. The men scrambled out of the trench and were startled to see a banshee standing in their way. The banshee wailed and instantly German bullets killed Daniel O'Conner.

2. The Amityville Horror

Actor James Brolin is certain there was an evil jinx on the film *The Amityville Horror,* in which he starred. He played surveyor George Lutz who, with his family, was driven from his home by a terrifying series of demonic happenings. The film was based on the best-selling book by Jay Anson, to whom the Lutz family told their nightmare story.

Brolin said: "On the first day of filming I stepped into the elevator in my apartment block and pressed the button for the lobby floor. Before we'd gone three floors it shuddered to a grinding, screeching halt, the lights flickered and I was plunged into frightening darkness. I screamed for help but nobody could hear me. It was an eerie, frightening experience. You imagine all sorts of hair-raising things in the silent darkness. My pleas bounced back like an echo. Those 30 minutes seemed an eternity."

The jinx hit again the next morning. "I'd been on the set less than one minute when I tripped over a cable and severely wrenched my ankle," said Brolin. "I hobbled around in pain for days."

The film recorded the horrifying events experienced by George and Kathleen Lutz and their three children after they moved to Long Island, New York, to a house, which had been the scene of a multiple murder in 1974.

Ronald Defoe, 23-year-old son of a wealthy car dealer, had drugged his parents, brothers and sisters at supper and at 3.15 a.m., he stalked from room to room shooting each victim in the back with a rifle.

He claimed in court that "voices" had ordered him to commit the crime. Defoe was sentenced to six consecutive life sentences.

For the Lutzes, the house's macabre history gave them the chance to buy a dream home at the bargain price of $80,000. Seen in the bright light of day, it was a beautiful, three-storeyed colonial-style residence, set on a well-kept lawn which sloped gently down to the bay, and its own boathouse. In the small middle-class community of Amityville, it was a showplace.

Soon after the family moved in they asked the local priest, Father Mancuso (played in the film by Rod Steiger) to bless the house. Author Anson wrote:

"The priest entered the house to begin his ritual. When he flicked the first holy water and uttered the words that accompany the gesture, Father Mancuso heard a masculine voice say with terrible clarity, 'Get out!'

"He looked up in shock, but he was alone in the room. Who or whatever had spoken was nowhere to be seen."

For the first two nights in their new home, the Lutzes were awakened by strange noises at 3.15 a.m. But the real horror began on the third night.

As usual, George Lutz checked that all doors and windows were locked before going to bed. The noises roused him again at 3.15, and this time he went downstairs to investigate.

He could not believe what he saw. The heavy, solid-wood front door had been wrenched open and was hanging by one hinge. With mounting terror he realised it had been forced from inside the house. The thick steel doorknob spindle was twisted, and the surrounding metal plate had been forced outwards.

From then on, the house seemed to have an evil life of its own, windows opened and closed at will and a bannister was wrenched from the staircase.

Two weeks after the front-door incident, George woke in the night to find his wife Kathleen floating above the bed. George pulled Kathleen down by her hair and switched on the light. He was looking not at his attractive young wife, but at a hideous vision.

Kathleen caught a glimpse of her reflection in a mirror and screamed:

"That's not me. It can't be me!" Her appearance changed slowly back to normal over the next six hours.

A few nights later Kathleen was in the sitting room with George when she looked up and saw two glowing red eyes at the darkened window. She and George hurried outside and found strange tracks in the snow. Kathleen told Anson: "The prints had been left by cloven hooves – like those of an enormous pig."

After only 28 days the Lutzes fled the dream house that had become a nightmare.

As they hurriedly gathered a few belongings, amid a series of unearthly noises, green slime oozed from the walls and ceiling and a sticky black substance dripped from the keyholes.

Because of the curse, the film men dared not use the actual house. They found an almost identical building in New Jersey. They knew only too well of the frightening things that had happened to people connected with the story.

A photographer went to take pictures of Anson immediately after photographing the Amityville house. While he was in the author's home, his car caught fire and billowed orange smoke as it stood empty with the engine switched off.

Anson himself told of terrifying events linked with his book. He said: "A woman to whom I loaned some early chapters took the manuscript home. She and two of her children were suffocated in a fire that night. The only item in the apartment that was not damaged by the fire was the manuscript.

"Another man put the manuscript in the trunk of his car and attempted to drive home. He drove through what he thought was a puddle. It turned out to be a 12-foot-deep hole into which his car slid. When the car was fished out the next day, the only dry object in it was the manuscript.

"And when my editor picked up the completed manuscript at my office, his car caught fire and he discovered that all the bolts on his engine had been loosened."

Anson himself suffered a heart attack, and his son and friend were nearly killed in a car smash.

The Lutzes are today alive and well in California, and planning another book about their experiences. Island house of horrors is now owned by James and Barbara Cromarty.

They say the place is not haunted.

Whatever the truth, the movie *The Amityville Horror,* will remain a chillingly realistic record of paranormal events. Director

Stuart Rosenberg says that he would not have taken on the project if it was just another horror film.

He insists, "My first reaction was that it wouldn't be my cup of tea. But I read Jay Anson's book – and it had the ring of truth about it."

3. The Demon Drummer

The horrific story of the demon drummer began mundanely when a beggar was hauled before a magistrate by the name of Mompesson in March 1661. The beggar was well-known in the district for playing a drum. He was found guilty of a minor crime and sent to jail. Mompesson confiscated the drum and took it home to Tedworth House, Wiltshire. The ghostly trouble began three nights later.

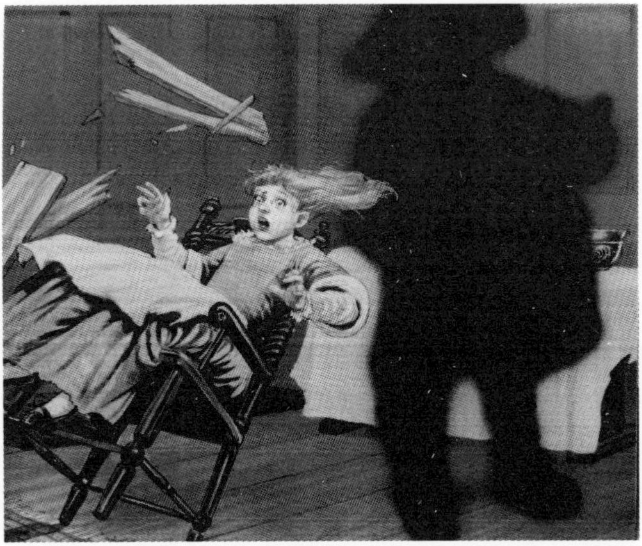

As the Mompesson family lay asleep, a terrific hammering noise woke them up. It sounded as if somebody was kicking the doors in the house. Though Mr. Mompersson searched the building, no intruder could be found. The next night the door-thumping occurred again. A few nights later, the banging noises echoed along a corridor and into the room where the beggar's drum was kept. There was a moment's silence. Then the drum began to play. A long roll sounded out and after that silence returned.

The next night the drum played again. As the days passed, the drum became more and more active. It floated through the air and played itself for long periods of time. While the drum played, other terrifying phenomenon frightened the family. Shoes and chairs were hurled across rooms. Floorboards were ripped up and the children had their hair pulled by invisible hands. On one occasion, the demon drummer became visible for a time. Its glowing red eyes scared a servant so much that he left the house immediately and never returned.

After several weeks of these upsetting phenomenon, Mr. Mompesson received a message from the beggar, who was now free from jail. The beggar demanded the return of his drum, saying that he was responsible for the disturbances. Far from returning the drum, Mompesson promptly re-arrested the man and charged him with witchcraft. The beggar was found guilty and transported to America. The dreadful drumming then suddenly stopped.

4. Accursed Blade

It sounds as if the story of the Herero knife, its gold handle studded with jewels, had come from the pen of a fiction writer, but not so. The knife carried a curse – at least 28 people suffered a violent death after coming into contact with it.

The story of the knife begins way back in 1917 when it came into the possession of a German army officer, Lieutenant Froelich. He believed that the chief of the African Herero tribe knew the whereabouts of a treasure trove. Froelich and three soldiers kidnapped the chief and his wife and tortured the woman with the knife until the chief was forced to tell that the fortune in gold was buried in a certain Kraal. The lieutenant led his three soldiers against the Kraal and slaughtered everyone in it. The officer then murdered two of his own men, his mind filled with greed.

But other natives had seen the massacre and followed Froelich and his companion as they drove off in a wagon loaded with the treasure. While they slept that night, the two Germans were killed and their bodies left with the wagon – and the treasure.

Twenty-five years passed and two gold prospectors chanced to camp on the spot. The sands had buried the treasure wagon and the two men, searching for firewood, came across the top of the wagon.

Mainly out of curiosity, the two men scooped away the sand and uncovered the two skeletons of Froelich and his companion and the gold – plus the tarnished knife.

The two men polished the knife up and took off into town to sell the gold. This done, they bought tickets for

Johannesburg the next day. But that night one of the men was killed in a drunken brawl.

The other man sold the knife to a firm of jewellers in Johannesburg, Cohen and Rosenblatt.

Cohen took the knife to show to his wife. A few days later the couple was killed by burglars who broke into the house.

Already 25 people had died after being connected with the knife but Cohen's son, to whom the dagger had passed, scoffed at the idea that it carried a curse. Some weeks later, while driving his new sports car, he spun off a straight road and crashed over a cliff. He was number 26. From now on no one wanted to own the dagger and it passed quickly from hand to hand.

One man, named Sturman, bought and displayed it on the wall of his home. A few days later he was killed by lightning.

The knife lay unclaimed amongst Sturman's effects until a wealthy American instructed his agent in Africa, Dark Nathan, to purchase it for him. Nathan bought it and quickly hurried to dispatch it at the Post Office, relieved to get rid of the accursed blade. As he walked out of the Post Office, Nathan was run down and killed by a lorry.

From that time nothing more has been heard of the Herero dagger. With such a reputation no one wishes to find it.

5. Nothing But Trouble

A curse is an invocation of destruction or evil, part of the accustomed armoury of the priest, magician, shaman or ill-wisher.

There do seem to be numerous cases of curse victims being totally sceptical of supernatural 'mumbo-jumbo', which nevertheless does nothing to save them from the effects.

Take the case of Robert Heinl Jr., a retired colonel in the US Marine Corps. From 1958 to 1963, he served in Haiti as chief of the US naval mission, while his wife studied the voodoo religion. Afterwards, back in the United States, they wrote *Written in Blood*, a history of Haiti that was openly critical of the ruling dynasty of Francois 'Papa Doc' Duvalier. Then they learned from a newspaper published by Haitian exiles that a curse had been placed on the book, probably after Papa Doc's death in 1971 by his widow, Simone.

At first, the Heinls were flattered that their book was thought to be worth cursing, but amusement soon turned to fear. First, the manuscript was lost on the way to the publishers, then it turned up four months later in a room the publishers never used. Meanwhile, the Heinls prepared another copy of the manuscript and sent it off for binding and stitching. The machine immediately broke down. A *Washington Post* reporter who was preparing to interview the authors was struck down with acute appendicitis. The colonel fell through a stage when he was delivering a speech, injuring his leg. And while walking near his home was suddenly – and severely – bitten by a dog.

The omens continued, two involving the number 22, which Papa Doc considered a magic number. Finally, on May 5, 1979, the Heinls were on holiday on St. Barthelemy Island, near Haiti, when the colonel dropped dead from a heart attack. His widow mused: 'There is a belief that the closer you get to Haiti, the more powerful the magic becomes.'

6. Zack's Curse

The old West had its share of ghost stories, but none is stranger than the tale of the steer branded "Murder". From 1890 to 1920, cowhands shuddered over the legend.

The story began in 1890 in Brewster County, Texas, where the brothers Zack and Gil Spencer were rounding up longhorn cattle. The two had always been close, but tempers frayed in the hectic roundup. Suddenly there was a dispute between them over a handsome steer with an enormous spread of horns.

"We could draw straws for him," Gil suggested.

"Or better yet, our guns," Zack roared, whipping his six-gun out of its holster and shooting his younger brother dead.

When his temper abated, Zack was grief-stricken. He sadly lifted his brother's body and placed it tenderly over the back of a horse. A thoughtless cowhand asked how the steer should be branded now.

“With the same kind of brand that’s on my hide,” Zack sobbed. “Brand him ‘Murder’ and cut him loose, and I hope to God he haunts the mesa for a 1,000 years!”

He buried his brother that afternoon and then killed himself.

A few months later, the branded steer began to appear in widely separate parts of the countryside. Amazingly, many who had even a passing glimpse of him were fated to kill or be killed.

A cowboy saw him and told his two best friends about it. When they accused him of lying, he shot them both. Hours after sighting the maverick steer, a small rancher killed his brother-in-law in a family argument.

A runaway boy lost all desire to be a gunman when he met the steer on a lonely trail. In the nearest cowtown, he tried to surrender his guns to the marshal. Tragically, the marshal misinterpreted the gesture and shot him down.

It was believed that the steer had died and had become a ghost whose restless hooves were taking it across all borders. The physical description had changed, too. The steer was now a bull.

Lon Allan, a Montana rancher, said in 1920, “The brand across him looked big and red and not healed up the way it ought to be, not haired over at all. It looked as raw and cruel in the moonlight as on the day they burned it into the critter.”

Allan had been a partner with his friend Cole Farrell in a small spread next to Faye Dow’s D-Down ranch. Dow wanted their land and one night called on Allan when he knew Farrell was in town. He managed to convince Allan that his friend was making love to his girl.

Crazed with jealousy, Allan crouched in a midnight ambush with a six-gun in his hand. At the sound of hoofbeats on the trail, he braced himself to kill. But the thing that blundered into the moonlight wasn't Cole Farrell's horse. It was the bull branded Murder.

In a wild panic, Allan sent four bullets crashing into the creature's skull. The apparition looked at him sadly and drifted away.

Faye Dow heard the shots and gleefully rushed to the scene. As the plot became evident, there was a shoot-out in which Allan was wounded and Dow died with two bullets in him.

In the strange trial that followed, Allan took the stand in his own defence. And in defence of the bull.

It was true, he said, that he'd seen the phantom and had killed a man moments later. But his partner was riding towards the ranch, and if it hadn't been for the bull he'd have killed the wrong man. The jury took ten minutes to acquit Allan.

The ghostly bull with the scarlet brand faded into history, for no one ever saw him again.

7. Ring of Death

When the silent film star, Rudolph Valentino, bought a silver ring set with a semi-precious stone, the jeweller told him it had a reputation for bringing bad luck to its owner. Valentino scoffed at the idea and wore the ring while filming his next film, *The Young Rajah*. The film was a box-office disaster.

The ring was put away for several years. After the success of two of his films, Valentino had forgotten about the curse on the ring and in 1926 he wore it again. Shortly afterwards, he fell ill and later died in New York.

A friend of Valentino's inherited the ring. She fell ill, but when she passed on the ring to a young artist named Russ Colombo she recovered from her illness almost immediately. While Colombo was wearing the ring, he was killed in a car accident. So was the next owner of the ring.

The ring was then stolen and the thief was spotted by a policeman. The policeman was an excellent shot and he fired a warning in the air. As he did so, his gun slipped – the burglar was killed by accident.

Because of its reputation the ring was placed in a bank. The bank, which had never been robbed before, was robbed twice. In the course of one robbery, several innocent members of the public were killed.

8. Papillon Hall

Papillon Hall stands to the west of Market Harborough, Leicestershire, England, between the villages of Lubenham and Theddingworth. David Papillon of French Huguenot descent built the hall in 1622-24 on the site once occupied by a "Lazar-House" in connection with Leicester Abbey. In the grounds was a holy well known as St. Mary's Well or by others as the "Everlasting Well". In 1629, David Papillon was appointed by King Charles I to superintend the redemption and sale of the crown jewels that had previously been pawned in Holland in order to satisfy a debt incurred to support the King's sister, the Queen of Bohemia.

In 1691 David Papillon II was born. This was the great-grandson of the hall's founder and where this story seems to begin. Little is documented about this David and it seems he lived a very secluded life until his marriage to Mary Keyser. However, local stories at the time ran riot about the man known to them as "Pamp". Deeply feared by local people, he was said to have strange hypnotic powers with an ability to "Fix" people, in effect causing a form of temporary paralysis with a single glance. There were also rumours of drunkenness and debauchery and the presence of a Spanish mistress kept locked away at the hall. The women often seen by locals walking around the grounds vanished without trace in or around 1715. David Papillon eventually left the hall sometime after 1717 following his marriage to his wife Mary and moved to Acrise in Kent. However he left strict instructions that certain objects should under no circumstances leave the hall.

Following David Papillon's rather hurried departure from the hall in 1717, he left behind certain items which he forbid to leave the hall or be sent on to him in Kent. One was the portrait of him that had been painted in 1715 by an unknown artist and other items including a pair of slippers. Although not confirmed, it is thought they were the property of David's mistress who had previously disappeared in 1715. It was also reported by one of Papillon's staff that he had heard his master speak of a curse on "these Dammed slippers". Over the years the hall was sold on to various people but always with the condition these objects remain within the house.

In 1866 Lord Hopetoun acquired the hall, which until now had remained seemingly untroubled. However, soon afterwards, family and staff heard strange knocking, bangs and voices. On one occasion it became so violent that the hall's entire staff gathered in the lobby with family members as the sound of wailing and furniture being thrown and slammed echoed from the drawing room. When enough courage was finally raised the door was opened but not a single item had been moved. After enquiries were made to the Rector of Lubenham, it followed that the hall's previous owner, the Bosworth family, had bequeathed the house's contents to their daughter, including the slippers and portrait. After tracing the beneficiary to nearby Leicester, the items were returned to the hall and the disturbance stopped. Again the house changed hands, this time to Thomas Halford. Undaunted by stories of curses and haunting, Halford loaned the slippers to the Paris Exhibition. Again violent disturbances flared almost immediately. Unable to redeem the shoes until the end of the exhibition, a whole year, the entire hall was vacated for the duration of their absence. Unable to cope with the constant occurrences, Halford sold the house in 1884 to C.W. Walker.

Aware of the stories concerning the Papillon articles, Walker commissioned a fireproof safe embedded within the wall for the safe-keeping of the slippers. Again all fell quiet. Walker lived peacefully at the hall for 19 years until the house was sold yet again to Captain Frank Bellville in 1903. Almost immediately after moving to Papillon Hall, Belville commissioned alterations by the world-renowned architect Sir Edward Lutyens. Work began that year with the slippers being sent to the family solicitor for safe-keeping. With work underway, a series of accidents began to occur with one builder being killed by falling masonry. The company declined the rest of the work and a new workforce was found. Shortly afterwards Belville was travelling to Market Harborough by horse and trap. The horse, for no apparent reason, bolted throwing the couple from the trap. His wife was unhurt but Belville sustained a fractured skull. A few days later the hall's stables were struck by lightning killing one of Belville's polo ponies. Once more the slippers returned. Belville, apparently distraught, locked away the slippers and threw the key into the hall's ornamental pond. Belville also wrote of being disturbed by Papillon's portrait, also commented on by previous owners as creating great unease and emitting an evil and hypnotic stare.

The hall remained in the Belville family for around 37 years until being requisitioned by the government around 1940 and subsequently occupied by members of the US Forces, in particular the 82nd Airborne Div., who eventually stumbled upon the slippers. Breaking open the safe, the slippers once again left the hall. This time as souvenirs. Although the fate of the particular airmen is unknown, the slippers eventually somehow returned to the hall. Unable to find a new occupier after the war, the main part of the hall was demolished in 1950. The slippers, however were claimed by none other than a Papillon descendent, at the time living in Colchester. David Papillon retained these things until his own death during the 1970s.

9. Retroactive Magic

While he was in the Congo in 1682, the Italian missionary Father Jerome Merolla da Sorrento heard a curious story demonstrating the sometimes fatal effects of superstitious fear. During a journey a young black man had spent the night at a friend's house, and in the morning the friend had prepared a wild hen for breakfast. This was a food that young people were forbidden to eat, by inviolable tribal custom, and the visitor asked his friend if the dish he had prepared was really wild hen. The host replied that it was not, and the young guest ate a hearty breakfast.

A few years later the two men met again, and the friend asked his former guest if he would eat a wild hen. No, he said, that was impossible – he had been solemnly warned by a magician never to eat that food. The friend laughed and asked why he should refuse to eat the dish now, when he had been perfectly happy to eat it before. As soon as the guest learned the truth about the breakfast his host had once served him, he began to tremble violently and within 24 hours was dead, the victim of his own fear.

10. The Mummy's Hand

Count Louis Hamon was famed as an occultist and psychic healer. He was often given exotic presents by grateful clients he had cured. But the oddest gift of all brought him nothing but trouble.

On a visit to Luxor, Egypt, in 1890, Hamon cured a prominent sheik of malaria. The sheik insisted that the healer accept a gruesome gift, the mummified right hand of a long-dead Egyptian princess.

Count Hamon's wife disliked the dry, shrivelled hand from the first. But her dislike turned to horror and revulsion when she heard the story behind it. In the seventeenth and last year of his reign, King Akhnaton of Egypt – the heretical father-in-law of Tutankhamun – quarrelled over religious matters with his daughter. And the king's vengeance was ghastly.

In 1357 BC, he had the girl raped and murdered by his priests. Afterwards they cut off her right hand and buried it secretly in the Valley of the Kings. The people of Egypt were appalled, for the girl would be barred from paradise because her body was not intact at burial.

Hamon would have turned the relic over to a museum, but could not find a curator willing to accept it. He locked it away in an empty safe in the wall of his London home.

In October 1922, he and his wife reopened the safe – and stood back in horror. The murdered girl's hand had changed. Shrivelled and mummified for 3,200 years, it had begun to soften with new flesh. The Countess screamed that it must be destroyed. Although he had never before been afraid of the unknown, Hamon agreed with her.

He insisted on only one thing; that the hand of the princess must have the best funeral they could give it. They were ready on the night of October 31, 1922. Halloween.

In a letter to his life-long friend, the archaeologist Lord Carnarvon, Hamon wrote that he laid the hand gently in the fireplace and read aloud a passage from the *Egyptian Book of the Dead.* As he closed the book there was a blast of thunder that rocked the house into total darkness. The door flew open with a sudden wind.

Hamon and his wife fell to the floor and lay there in the sudden glacial cold. Lifting their eyes, they saw the figure of a woman. In Hamon's account, "She wore the royal apparel of old Egypt, with the serpent of the House of Pharaohs glittering on her tall headdress". The woman's right arm ended in a raw stump.

The apparition bent over the fire and then was gone as suddenly as it had appeared. The severed hand had vanished with it, and was never seen again.

Four days later, Hamon read that the Carnarvon expedition had discovered Tutankhamun's tomb and that they would enter it in spite of the ancient warning emblazoned at the threshold.

From the room in the hospital where he and his wife were under treatment for severe shock, Hamon sent his old friend a letter begging him to reconsider.

He wrote, "I know now the ancient Egyptians had knowledge and power of which today we have no comprehension. In the name of God, I beg you to take care."

Carnarvon ignored the letter and soon afterwards he was dead from an infected mosquito bite. One by one, members of the expedition followed him to the grave in what became known as the Curse of the Pharaohs.

11. God of Good Luck?

The year was 1928. The city, Kobe, Japan. A middle-aged English couple, the C. J. Lamberts, stood in front of a junk shop window. "That's what I'd like," said Marie Lambert, pointing to a tiny statuette of a half-naked fat man seated on a cushion. She recognised the laughing man as Ho-tei, the Japanese god of good luck. "Let's find out what he costs," said her husband, as they walked into the shop. They were pleasantly surprised to find that the figurine was cheap, even though it was made of ivory. It seemed almost too good to be true. Back on their cruise ship the Lamberts examined their purchase closely. The statuette had the creamy colour of old ivory and was beautifully carved. As far as they could see, its only minor imperfection was a small hole underneath, plugged neatly with an ivory peg. If the carver had used the base of an elephant's tusk for the statue, which was possible, the tiny hole would be natural as the point where the nerve of the animal's tooth had ended. Altogether, the statue seemed to be one of those rare bargains that tourists dream about. The Lamberts hoped the presence of the "Laughing Buddha," as Ho-tei is sometimes called, would insure good luck for the remainder of their voyage.

Ho-tei was originally a 6th century Buddhist monk who devoted his life to helping the poor, taking special care of children. Statuettes of Ho-tei, who later became a god, show him holding in his right hand a string of beads or a fan, and in his left hand a sack. Sometimes a small child is hanging onto his back or sitting on his shoulder, illustrating a legend that he once carried a child to safety across a dangerously flooded river. The legend of St. Christopher, who features on many good luck charms in the West as the protector of travellers, is believed to be a Christianised version of the legend of Ho-tei.

Marie Lambert packed the statuette in one of her suitcases. On the second day out, en route to Manila, the next scheduled stop, Mrs. Lambert began to suffer from a toothache. The ship's doctor prescribed painkillers, but they did little good. Once in Manila, both Lamberts contracted an unpleasant fever whose chief symptom was pain in all the joints, and Marie Lambert had to delay her visit to a dentist. When she finally got to one, his drill slipped during treatment and drove through the nerve of her tooth, increasing her pain instead of curing it.

On the next lap of the voyage, which took the ship to Australia, Mr. Lambert in turn was prostrated with an agonising toothache. While in Cairns he went to a doctor, who told him there was nothing wrong with his teeth. In fact, the ache had stopped while he was at the dentist's. It started again as soon as he returned to his cabin. Two days later he consulted another dentist, and the same thing happened. Finally, in Brisbane he desperately ordered a dentist to start pulling out his teeth and to keep on pulling until the pain stopped. When the first tooth came out, the pain went away. However, it started again as soon as Lambert returned to the ship. He had not noticed that the Ho-tei figurine was in his suitcase at the time his toothache started.

In Sydney, the Lamberts left their luggage checked, and the toothache ceased. On the voyage to New Zealand the luggage was in their cabin only once, when they repacked; Lambert's toothache started again. When the luggage went into the hold, the pain stopped. While on shore in New Zealand he had no toothache, and there was only one bout of toothache on the continuation trip to Chile – when the Lamberts repacked their luggage in the cabin.

In the United States the couple visited Lambert's mother, who was so delighted with Ho-tei that they made her a present of the little god. When her excellent teeth started aching a few hours later, she handed back the gift saying that she felt it was "bad medicine." In spite of this hint about the statuette's ill effects on its owners, the Lamberts did not connect Ho-tei with their own toothaches till they were on their way across the Atlantic to Britain. A fellow passenger, who was interested in ivory, borrowed the figurine overnight to show her husband.

In the morning she mentioned that she and her husband had both had toothaches. The Lamberts then thought about their toothaches, and realised that it had always occurred when Ho-tei was in their cabin. Marie Lambert wanted to throw the statuette overboard at once, but her husband was afraid that the god might retaliate by rotting every tooth in their heads. So they brought Ho-tei back to London with them.

Lambert took the figure to an oriental art shop and showed it to the Japanese manager, who immediately offered to buy it. Lambert explained that he could not take money for it, and described the troubles it seemed to have caused. The manager sent for an old kimono-clad Japanese, and the two men examined the statuette carefully. From what they then told him, Lambert gathered that his Ho-tei had been a temple god. In the East, the statues of such gods are sometimes given "souls" in the form of small medallions hidden inside them. That probably explained the ivory plug in the base of the figure. The old man placed Ho-tei in a shrine at the end of the shop and lit joss sticks in front of it. Then with an expression of awe, he bowed Lambert out of the shop.

12. Rocks of Wrath

During the summer of 1977, airline vice-president Ralph Loffert, of Buffalo, New York State, USA, his wife and four children visited the Hawaiian volcano Mauna Loa. While there they collected some stones from the volcano despite a warning from locals that this would anger the volcano goddess, Pele. Some claim to have seen Pele, who traditionally appears to warn of imminent eruptions. Shortly after they returned home,

Mauna Loa erupted. Within a few months one of the Loffert boys, Todd, developed appendicitis, had knee surgery and broke his wrist; another son Mark, sprained an ankle and broke his arm; another son Don, caught an eye infection and had to wear glasses; and the daughter, Rebecca, lost two front teeth in a fall. In July 1978, the Lofferts sent the stones to a friend in Hawaii who was asked to return them to the volcano. But the disasters continued – Mark hurt his knee, Rebecca broke three more teeth, Dan fractured a hand bone, while Todd dislocated an elbow and fractured his wrist again. Mark then confessed that he still had three stones. They were returned – and the troubles ceased.

Mrs. Allison Raymond of Ontario, Canada, and her family also took some stones away from the volcano. She told reporters:

"My husband was killed in a head-on car crash and my mother died of cancer. My younger son was rushed to hospital with a pancreas condition that's slowly getting worse. Then he broke his leg. My daughter's marriage nearly broke up and it was only when I posted the rocks back that our luck improved."

Despite warning, Nixon Morris, a hardwood dealer from El Paso, Texas, took a Mauna Loa stone home. He fell off the roof, lightning struck an antenna and ruined several home appliances, and his wife fell ill with a mysterious infection that left her knee swollen.

Then Morris broke a hip and thigh when he fought with a burglar in their house. The family cat was sleeping under the bonnet of his wife's car when she started the engine and stripped off its fur down one side. Then Morris's grand-daughter fell and broke her arm in two places.

Morris said he had broken the rock in two and given a piece to a friend, adding: 'He brought the rock back to me after he wrecked four cars in less than two years, and he'd never before had a wreck in his life'. In March 1981 Morris sent the rocks back.

Jon Erickson, a naturalist at the Volcanoes National Park in Hawaii, said he receives up to 40 packages of rock a day from frightened tourists who have returned home.

13. Curse of the Vengeful Midget

Police have never solved one of the most bizarre murders in criminal history – for the killer was a dead woman. The roots of the crime go back to the 1870s, when Miss Ada Danforth and her little ward, Fanchon Moncare, regularly cruised between France and New York.

Miss Danforth explained that Fanchon was an orphan whose parents had died in a fire. On her 18th birthday she would inherit a fortune, but meanwhile Ada was her legal guardian.

Fanchon would curtsy adorably to any inquiring passenger and skip away with her doll. But back in their stateroom, the child's masquerade ended. Fanchon's cherubic face would twist into a mask of evil. She would flay her "guardian" with the gutter language acquired from 3 years of hard living .....from her early days as a circus midget to her present career as a thief and smuggler.

In spite of the quarrels, the partnership was successful. While Ada attended to the baggage, little Fanchon – whose real name was Estelle Ridley – would dance through customs barriers still cradling her cherished doll. And no one ever dreamed of stopping her.

Afterwards, the pair would take a cab to New York's Chinatown, where Wing To, an elderly friend, waited to receive them. In the back room, the head of the doll was unscrewed and a fortune in gems spilled out – the harvest of several months' larceny on the Continent.

The business might have gone on for years but for one thing – Fanchon entered into a deadly feud with a beautiful rival, Magda Hamilton. According to police records, both woman were vying for the affections of Dartney Crawley, a high stakes gambler.

Magda violated all the underworld taboos by going to the police as an informer, and the partners in crime found a reception committee waiting for them when they next docked in New York. For the first time ever, little Fanchon's doll was inspected, and minutes later the pair were en route to the notorious Tombs prison.

The midget, who had an impressive criminal record, was sentenced to life imprisonment. Ada, 10 years younger, was jailed as an accessory for 20 years.

It was Fanchon who provided the most dramatic moment of the trial. When she saw the gloating Magda sitting in the packed courtroom, the midget sprang to her feet, made a shrill vow that she would one day kill her betrayer.

Triumphantly, Magda married Dartney Crawley. He deserted her six months later to try his luck in a California mining venture. But the divorce settlement was generous, and Magda was very comfortably off. Her prosperity grew through shrewd investments, and she became a prominent figure in New York cafe society.

Fanchon was all but forgotten by everyone.....but Magda Hamilton. One morning she burst into police headquarters and viciously cursed the officers for not letting her know that Fanchon had escaped.

She had awakened from a heavy sleep, she said, to find the midget in her bedroom. Fanchon still wore her childish finery and clutched a big china doll. But she was now a bent and withered hag, grinning with toothless gums.

Magda screamed and fled into the bathroom where she locked the door and cowered for the rest of the night.

The hysterical Magda now insisted on adequate police protection until the little monster was recaptured.

A bemused police sergeant produced a week-old copy of the New York Sun.

He pointed to a short item on the back page reporting that Fanchon Moncare had hanged herself in her cell.

That afternoon, Magda Hamilton booked passage for Europe on a Cunard liner. Since the ship was to leave the next day, she had a farewell dinner with a friend and then went home.

Next day the servants found her trunks neatly packed. But there would be no ocean voyage for Magda. The woman was sprawled half-naked on the bed, her eyes protruded and there was congealed blood at the corners of her mouth. According to the medical examiner, she literally drowned in her own blood. The membrane of her throat was ruptured as if some heavy object had been rammed into it with savage force.

The murder weapon was never found. But there was a clue of sorts. Lodged in Magda's bloody mouth were several hairs – similar to those found on the head of a child's china doll.

14. The Guinness Family

While a curse is a conscious invocation of misfortune against others, a jinx is merely a bringer of bad luck – why it starts is anybody's guess. Jinxes may be curses in disguise, unknown to the victims. It could even be that someone who suffers a series of inexplicable misfortunes comes to believe himself to be jinxed – and so unconsciously brings about further disasters.

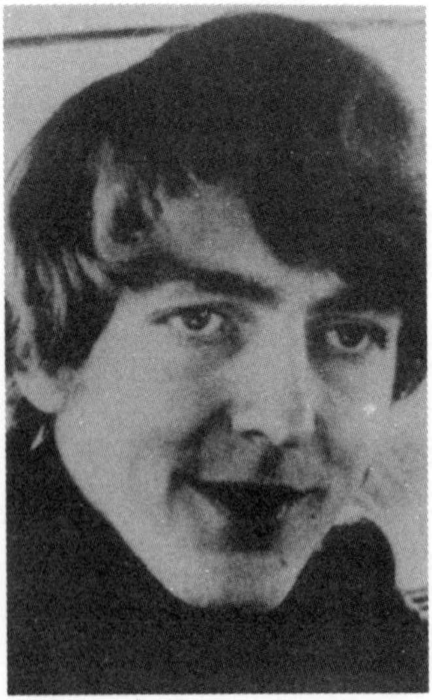

No one has come up with an explanation for the misfortunes of the Guinness brewery family. In 1978 they suffered four deaths in as many months: in May, Lady Henrietta Guinness plunged to her death from an aqueduct in Spoleto, Italy; in June another Guinness heiress drowned in a bath while trying to inject herself with heroin. Also in June, Major Dennys Guinness was found dead in Hampshire with an empty pill bottle by his side. In August, John Guinness, then an aide to British Prime Minister James Callaghan, survived a head-on collision in Norfolk, but his four-year-old son was killed and another son seriously injured. Lady Henrietta's cousin, Tara Browne, had died in a car crash in Chelsea in 1966.

15. 'Curse Aria'

There is a jinxed aria in Halevy's *Charles VI,* which was premiered at the Opera Comique in Paris in 1852. As the celebrated tenor Maffiani sang 'Oh God, smash him', meaning the traitorous villain, he lifted his eyes to the ceiling. One of the stage hands immediately toppled to his death from a perch aloft. Maffiani was inconsolable, and the following morning the newspapers were calling it the 'Curse Aria'. On the next night when he sang it he fixed his eyes on an empty box. Suddenly, the curtains of the box parted and a man taking his seat swayed and toppled to his death. On the third night the tenor sang the aria staring at the floor, but a musician in the orchestra pit played off-key. Maffiani glared at him and he died of a heart attack.

Further performances were cancelled, but in 1858 Napoleon III asked Halevy to stage *Charles VI* for him. On the night before the performance, Napoleon and Eugenie narrowly escaped bombs hurled by Italian revolutionaries. The opera was cancelled and has never been staged since.

16. Curse of the Hope Diamond

Tales of romance and menace have been attached to many of the world's large gemstones, but none has a more romantic and sinister aura than the great Hope Diamond. It is said that everyone who has ever possessed the diamond had been cursed with extreme bad luck. That is something of an exaggeration, but the story is still an extraordinary one.

What was to become the Hope Diamond first appears in history in the seventeenth century when a French trader named John Baptiste Tavernier brought a large, blue, 112.50-carat diamond from India. Tavernier would not say where he got the diamond, but according to rumour it was stolen from the eye of an idol in the temple of Rama-Sita near Mandalay. There was also a rumour that the god would revenge himself on anyone who possessed the stolen diamond.

Tavernier sold the diamond to the only man in France who could truly afford it, King Louis XIV. The merchant himself ultimately seems to have suffered severe financial reverses, and he died unexpectedly during a trip to Russia.

The king had the diamond cut into a heart shape, and at that time it was called the French Blue. If there was a curse on the diamond, it didn't trouble Louis XIV, for he was France's most powerful and longest-lived monarch. The diamond passed down through the royal family to King Louis XVI, who gave it to his wife, Queen Marie Antoinette. Both the king and queen lost their thrones and their heads during the French Revolution. A close friend of the queen's, Princess de Lamballe, who often borrowed the diamond, was said to have been torn to pieces by an angry mob.

The diamond was apparently stolen during the Revolution and recut. Part of it reappeared rather mysteriously in London, now reduced to a mere 44.50 carats. It was purchased by banker Henry Thomas Hope, who gave the gem the name by which it is now known.

Hope himself never seems to have been afflicted by any particular ill fortune. After Hope's death, the diamond passed to other members of the family, but only one ever complained about it. She was May Yohe, a singer who married Lord Francis Hope. The couple was divorced, and the ex-singer died in poverty in 1938. She always blamed the diamond for her ill luck.

But by that time the diamond had long passed out of the Hope family. It was sold in 1901 to a jeweller who went bankrupt, and then to another jeweller who shot himself. The diamond's next owner was a dissolute Russian nobleman who shot his showgirl lover while she was onstage and later was reportedly stabbed to death by a group of Russian revolutionaries.

The next owner was a Greek jeweller who fell off a cliff. The diamond was then sold to Sultan Abdul Hamid of Turkey. The Turkish empire was crumbling, and the sultan himself was going mad; for these reasons he got the nickname "Abdul the Damned." Ultimately the sultan was deposed, and the diamond passed through the hands of several dealers until it was acquired by the famous French jeweller Pierre Cartier, who in turn sold it to Edward B. McLean, heir to an American newspaper fortune, and his independently wealthy wife Evalyn.

It was with the McLean family that the idea of a curse on the Hope Diamond was really established. Shortly after purchasing the diamond, McLean's mother died; so did two of the servants in the McLean household. Edward McLean himself seems to have been rather wary of the gem, but Evalyn McLean loved it and haughtily dismissed all notion of a curse. She often wore the diamond, now set in a necklace.

By far the most tragic and extraordinary death in the McLean family was that of ten-year-old Vinson. The boy had been called the hundred-million-dollar baby because of the huge sum of money he was due to inherit. Vinson was usually very carefully watched, but one day he slipped away from the servants, ran out in front of the family home in Washington, D.C., and was instantly struck and killed by a car. Since the boy was usually so thoroughly protected, this seemed to be a case of extraordinarily bad luck, or worse.

The McLean marriage was never a happy one and ended in divorce. McLean himself had always been a heavy drinker, and the divorce shattered his fragile mental stability. He was committed to a mental institution, where he died.

Still, Evalyn McLean refused to part with the diamond. When Charles Lindbergh's son was kidnapped, she tried to use the Hope Diamond to help raise ransom money. The attempt was unsuccessful.

In 1946, the McLean's only daughter died as a result of an overdose of sleeping pills. The newspapers recalled that at her wedding five years earlier, she had worn the Hope Diamond.

Evalyn McLean died a year later, but she was quite old and there was nothing unusual or untimely about her death. To the end she firmly rejected any notion of a curse.

The McLean gems, including the Hope Diamond, were purchased by the famous New York jeweller Harry Winston for about one million dollars. Winston put the famous diamond on display in New York and elsewhere for several years and then decided to donate it to the nation.

Winston took the unusual step of sending the diamond to the Smithsonian Institution by ordinary parcel post. He paid about $150 for insurance on the package, but otherwise took no extra precautions. Winston said he had no second thoughts about sending one of the world's most valuable diamonds through the mail.

The package arrived safely, and the great blue diamond is now one of the most popular exhibits in the Smithsonian. Exhibited along with the diamond is the package in which it was sent. Some have suggested, probably not seriously, that the diamond must have put a curse on the postal service from which it has never been released.

While many of those who did own the diamond do seem to have been unlucky, many others such as Louis XIV, Evalyn McLean, Harry Winston, and Henry Hope himself do not seem to have experienced any extraordinary bad luck. In addition, some of the stories told about the diamond, particularly about its early history, simply may not be true. The diamond changed hands many times, and often buyers and sellers wished to keep their identities secret, so it is impossible to be sure who actually owned the diamond. Of course, once the Hope Diamond got the reputation of being cursed, anything bad that happened to anyone who was even remotely connected with it was blamed on the curse.

The story of the curse of the Hope Diamond is so dramatically satisfying that it will probably be circulated forever.

17. Living on the Run

The *kundela* is used by the Aborigines for initiation ceremonies, against enemies, and against those who have broken tribal laws. Within those spheres its power is awesome. There seems to be only one instance of a man surviving after being condemned to die by the bone without the antidote of white man's medicine.

The man, Alan Webb, a full-blooded Aborigine of the Arunta tribe, had shot a fellow tribesman during a struggle over a rifle. In April 1969, the court found that Webb had been attacked and that the rifle had gone off accidentally. He was declared not guilty of the man-slaughter charge. Outside the courtroom, after the verdict had been returned, Webb was met by a tribal delegation. The white men's court was irrelevant, he was told, and he would have to stand trial before his peers among the Arunta.

Webb knew very well what the tribe's verdict would be. He had killed a member of his own tribe; therefore, he must die. He promptly left Alice Springs and was sentenced to death *in absentia* by the Aruntas.

This time the *kurdaitcha* had a more difficult task than usual. Their quarry was driving a van and living in it with his wife, two children, and three dogs. He slept with a rifle at his side, ready to be awakened at any moment by the barking of the dogs.

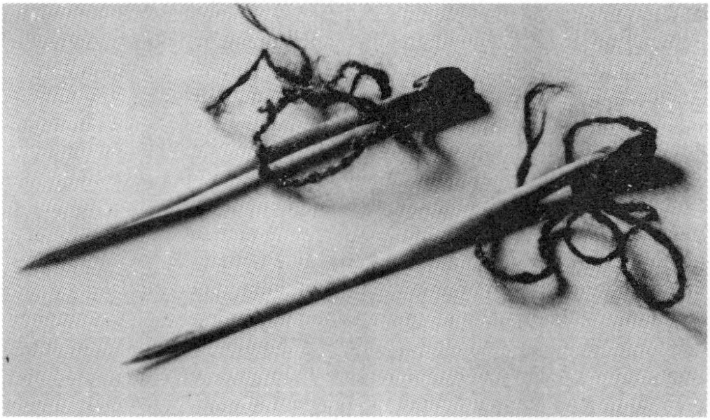

By 1976, the date of the last available information, Alan Webb had managed to evade the *kurdaitcha* for seven years, earning his living doing odd jobs and moving on whenever he heard that the death squad was coming his way. It is improbable that anyone has survived an Aborigine death sentence for a longer period. But Webb knew – and perhaps still knows – that the *kurdaitcha* would never abandon their pursuit. And although he spent his life on the fringe of white society, he realised that if his hunters ever came close enough to point the *kundela,* he would be as good as dead – killed, without trace of injury, by nothing more substantial than a spear of thought.

18. Almost Immune to Death

"If I am killed by common assassins, and especially by my brothers the Russian peasants, you ...... have nothing to *fear,*" wrote the "mad monk" Grigori Yefimovich Rasputin in December 1916 to his protector, Czar Nicholas II of Russia.

"But if I am murdered by Boyars (nobles), and if they shed my blood, their hands will remain soiled with my blood.... Brothers will kill brothers and they will kill each other and..... there will be no nobles in the country."

Rasputin, a filthy, rude-mannered, lecherous, hard-drinking peasant renowned for his hypnotic powers and healing skills, was the most feared and detested person in Russia because of his sway over the royal family. The czar and especially the czar's wife, the empress Alexandra, who believed he had miraculously saved the life of their haemophiliac son, were devoted to him.

In 1914 Rasputin had survived being knifed in the stomach by a peasant woman. Now, even as he wrote of his anticipated murder, several palace noblemen led by Prince Felix Yusupov were busy plotting it.

Inviting Rasputin to Yusupov's palace the night of December 29, 1916, they arranged that he should be the first to arrive, and laid out wine and cake for him. While he awaited the others, he helped himself generously to both, not suspecting that the refreshments were loaded with potassium cyanide. When Yusupov arrived and found his guest unaffected by the cyanide, he shot him in the back. Rasputin crumpled to the floor and was pronounced dead. A while later the conspirators returned to pick up the corpse and take it to the Neva River. But Rasputin sprang to life and, crawling on his hands and knees, pursued the terrified Yusupov up a flight of stairs. Shot twice more, the "monk" fell.

Certain that he was finally dead, the nobles kicked and battered him, took his body to the river, smashed a hole in the ice, and shoved him into the frigid water. To their disbelief Rasputin was still breathing as they did so. When his body was retrieved two days later, his right hand was found upon his chest with three fingers in a sign of benediction.

His predictions of what would follow his death and his curse on his murderers were soon realised with the Russian Revolution of 1917.

19. The Witch with the Wicked Eyes

Molly was her name. "Evil eye" spells were her game. She prowled through dark alleys of St. Louis during the early years of the 19th century, cackling like a mad loon and claiming the power to cast deadly spells by a glance of her bloodshot eyes.

"She was an ugly wench. Her long, stringy hair was filthy. Her face was misshapen, pockmarked, and often covered with running sores," an Eastern journalist wrote. "Her reputation as a witch with the evil eye started in April, 1833, in a rowdy riverfront tavern...."

A new arrival in St. Louis from New Orleans, the ugly hag shuffled into the tavern. "Who'll buy a bit of gin for an old lady," she simpered.

The patrons were indifferent to her pleas. The inn-keeper was less calm. He reached beneath the bar and brandished a menacing club at his unwanted visitor. "Get back to your grave, you ghoul," he shouted.

"It's the devil's eye for you," Molly said. Her voice dripped with burning hatred. A convulsive shudder racked her body. She stiffened into a rigid stance. Her split, parched lips chanted an ancient witch's incantation. A bloodshot orb focussed on the menacing bartender.

Incredibly, the bartender dropped the club, clutched at his heart, and slumped to the floor. Several customers rushed to his aid. "He's dead," was their rapid diagnosis. They turned to see the evil, leering face of the frightening hag.

"Here, take these bottles and be gone," snapped a customer. Avoiding her eyes, he hastily shoved several bottles of gin across the bar.

News of the uncanny spell and the bartender's death quickly spread through the city. It could have been a coincidence. Perhaps the innkeeper died from a natural heart attack. Yet despite their rationalisations, few people dared to test the dark powers supposedly possessed by the old hag.

Within hours, she was tagged the "Devil's Daughter" and "Empress of the evil eye." Shopkeepers paid Molly to not look upon their businesses. Mothers pressed presents upon the old crone. People with real or imaginary enemies paid handsomely for the power of her evil eye.

"My wife has a lover and..." lamented a cuckolded husband.

"Bring me something that belongs to him, and I'll fashion a powerful *juju* doll," Molly cackled.

"Are you certain it will work?" the anxious husband inquired.

"I learned my trade from the best voodoo queens in New Orleans," snapped Molly, sipping a tumbler of gin. "Hurry! Bring the thing so I can make the doll."

Whispered rumours said the lover died within a month after Molly, the witch, fashioned the doll. Streams of anxious wives, husbands, and hopeful lovers sought to purchase her dark powers. Molly claimed there was nothing beyond her powers. "I am a servant of the dark one," she proclaimed.

Molly prospered in St. Louis for two years. She charged dearly for her services and spent the shiny gold pieces on bottles of booze. Her reign came to an end in a grimy, muddy alley in the roughest part of the rowdy frontier city. The police discovered her body one morning. Her filthy, uncombed hair was reddened with blood where a powerful club had cracked her skull. A stake had been driven through her heart. A wooden cross lay on the crumpled body.

20. Princess of Death

Egyptologist Douglas Murray neither liked nor trusted the dishevelled American who sought him out in Cairo in 1910. The man had a furtive manner and appeared to be in the final stages of disease. But Murray, a refined Briton, could not resist the blandishments of his disreputable visitor – for the American was offering him the most priceless find of his career.

It was the mummy-case of a high princess in the temple of Ammon-Ra, who was supposed to have lived in Thebes in 1600 BC. The outside of the case bore the image of the princess, exquisitely worked in enamel and gold. The case was in an excellent state of preservation.

An avid collector, Murray couldn't resist. He drew a cheque on the Bank of England and took immediate steps to have the mummy-case shipped to his London home. The cheque was never cashed. The American died that evening. Murray learned from another Egyptologist in Cairo why the price had been so reasonable.

The princess from Ammon-Ra had held high office in the powerful Cult of the Dead, which had turned the fertile Valley of the Nile into a place only of death. Inscribed on the walls of her death chamber she had left a legacy of misfortune and terror for anybody who despoiled her resting place.

Murray scoffed at the superstition until three days later. That was when he went on a shooting expedition up the Nile and the gun he was carrying exploded mysteriously in his hand. After weeks of agony in hospital, his arm had to be amputated above the elbow.

On the return voyage to England, two of Murray's friends died "from unknown causes". Two Egyptian servants who had handled the mummy-case also died within a year.

Back in London, Murray found that the mummy-case had arrived. When he looked at it, the carved face of the princess "seemed to come alive with a stare that chilled the blood".

Although he had made up his mind to get rid of it, a woman friend convinced him that he should give it to her. Within weeks, the woman's mother died, her lover deserted her, and she was stricken with an undiagnosed "wasting disease". When she instructed her lawyer to make her will, he insisted on returning the mummy-case to Douglas Murray.

By now a broken wreck of a man, Murray wanted no part of it. He presented it to the British Museum, but even in that cold and scientific institution, the mummy-case was to become notorious. A photographer who took pictures of it immediately dropped dead. An Egyptologist in charge of the exhibit was also found dead in his bed.

Disturbed by the newspaper stories, the board of the museum met in secret. There was a unanimous vote to ship the mummy-case to a New York museum, which had agreed to accept the gift provided it was handled without publicity and sent by the safest possible means.

The case was to be shipped by the prestigious new vessel making her maiden voyage from Southampton to New York that month. All arrangements were successfully completed. But the mummy-case never reached New York. It was in the cargo hold of the "unsinkable" *Titanic* when she carried 1503 people to their doom on April 15, 1912.

21. The Haunted Ship *Ivan Vassili*

One of the most terrifying and shocking true ghost stories in history took place on a Russian freighter called the *Ivan Vassili.*

The *Ivan Vassili* was not a typical cursed or jinxed ship. There was nothing unusual or spectacular about her. She was built in St. Petersburg in 1897 to transport freight across the Baltic Sea to the Gulf of Finland. She was driven by a single triple-expansion steam engine. Her bunkers carried enough coal to take her 2500 miles at a speed of eight knots. She was made of riveted iron plates, while her deck and superstructure were wood. She had a record of reliability and stability to the point of being boring. No mishaps took place on her during the first five years that she plied the sea. Then everything changed overnight, and she became a sailor's worst nightmare of calamity and death.

In 1903, when the Russian government prepared for war with Japan, her role changed suddenly. She was ordered to carry a cargo of war materials to Vladivostok in advance of the Russian warships.

The steamer cut through the North Sea, the Atlantic, and south along the west coast of Africa, coaling in Capetown. Then she moved north along the east coast of Africa and Zanzibar, topping off her bunkers and taking on extra sacks of coal for the upcoming leg across the Indian Ocean.

Soon the nightmare would begin for the crew would realise that they'd taken on more than coal.

Everything was business as usual as the ship left the port and took to sea, but the crew suddenly felt that a presence was on board. Something just didn't feel right. No one knew exactly what the presence was, but everyone was certain that some sort of invisible entity was among them. When it was near, the men felt that something was watching them, and they would feel a sudden chill in the air.

This went on for a few days before the danger of the situation heightened and the entity began extracting an alarming toll on the crew.

One night before the change of watch, the men on deck saw the apparition. It looked human, but its features were impossible to make out. It was misty, glowing, and luminous as it strolled across the deck and disappeared behind a lifeboat.

The men were understandably shocked. Still, nothing remarkable happened until the ship reached the Port Arthur military base in China where the crew intended to refuel the ship.

On the night before the ship entered port, a crew member suddenly let loose with a horrifying scream that sent everyone into a panic. The crew literally went berserk, and a wild melee ensued, the men having no idea what they were doing as they beat each other and themselves. This episode ended with seaman Alec Govinski hurling himself into the murky black waves to his death. Afterwards, the other men collapsed to the deck, and everything returned to normal.

The ship resumed its journey to Vladivostok, and the crew was relieved when nothing unusual happened during the first and second day at sea. But then all hell broke loose again. On the third day, the crew went on a screaming, fighting, hysteric rampage. A few minutes later, they collapsed on the deck like before only to learn that another shipmate had thrown himself overboard to his death.

When the ship finally reached Vladivostok, twelve crew members abandoned ship. They were so afraid of whatever was aboard the vessel, that they couldn't get away from it fast enough and even attempted to escape before the cargo hatches were opened. Unfortunately for them, they were quickly rounded up like cattle and returned to the vessel where they were kept under armed surveillance.

The anxiety on the ship must have been high as the cargo

was unloaded; nevertheless, the *Ivan Vassili* was put to sea again on a voyage south to Hong Kong.

In no time, this leg of the trip erupted into yet another nightmare. Another hysterical frenzy occurred and another crew member killed himself. The next night, there was a repeat performance, resulting in another crew member's death. During the third episode, a stoker reportedly died of fear.

Then, just as the ship reached the port of Hong Kong, Captain Sven Andrist flung himself overboard and downed.

This time nothing could stop the crew members from deserting when the ship docked. The entire crew, except Second Officer Christ Hansen and five Scandinavian seamen, fled.

Either dedicated to duty or unfazed by the tragedies, Hansen, took over as captain and hired a new crew for the ship, and the steamer set out again, this time towards Sydney, Australia, to pick up a cargo of wool.

To Hansen's relief, the voyage south was uneventful – that was until just before they reached Sydney. Then Hansen suddenly had an urge to kill himself, took out his revolver, and shot himself to death.

In Sydney, even before the dock lines were secure, the crew started abandoning the ship – all except boatswain Harry Nelson.

Nelson set about finding another captain, one who didn't believe in ghosts or superstitions. He found his man, but it took four months to find another crew. By then, word had gotten around and no sailor in his right mind wanted to sail on the death ship.

The steamer was put to sea again; its destination, San Francisco. The trip went smoothly until a week later when the crew was set into a screaming melee again. This time, two seaman went totally mad and had to be confined below decks. In the morning, they were both found dead.

The next day, the new and sceptical captain, put a revolver in his mouth and pulled the trigger.

Following the latest round of tragedy, the crew, including Nelson, refused to continue with the voyage, and they turned the vessel around with the intent to return to Vladivostok. When the *Ivan Vasilli* arrived in the Russian city, the entire crew, including Nelson walked off the ship.

The men were offered rewards, incentives, and all kinds of bonuses for returning to the ship, but nothing would convince them to get back on the vessel. Not one of them wanted any part of the ship. No other sailor did either. Watchmen were unwilling to even get close to her – much less spend a night aboard her. And so the diabolical vessel sat in port, abandoned, for many years.

Ultimately, the sailors of Vladivostok decided that fire was the only way to destroy the evil entity that haunted the ship, and so in the winter of 1907, on a clear starry night, they sat it aflame. In dozens of small boats, they watched, cheering, as flames devoured the ship. Some even sang as the fiery bridge engulfed the ship. They cheered its demise, toasting the occasion with vodka as the iron skin buckled. Cast off from her moorings, she was dragged out to sea by a tugboat.

She still smouldered the next day and began rolling to starboard until she flipped over on her side and started to slide beneath the water. Those who watched swore that before the ship went under, an eerie scream emanated from the hulk.

No one ever knew what or who the evil entity was.

22. The Song of Death

In mid-April 1956, in Arnhem Land, Australia, a young Aborigine named Lya Wulumu fell sick and was taken by plane to a hospital in Darwin. He was unable to eat or drink because, although he tried, he could not swallow. There was, however, no apparent cause for his malady. Examinations, including X-rays, blood tests, and spinal taps, revealed nothing unusual.

What was going on in the victim's mind was another matter. He asked an attending Methodist minister to pray for him because, as he said, "me bin sung and me finish." The singing to which Wulumu referred is a form of ritual execution practiced by his people. In his case, a group of women were requested by his mother-in-law to sing him to death, perhaps in reprisal for some taboo that he had broken.

To inaugurate the ritual the women stole Wulumu's spear and throwing stick *(woomera)* and put them in a ceremonial log. Then they sang the songs that are believed to put the curse of death on the owner of the captured objects. After the singing, his club (*nullanulla*) was displayed in a treetop to signify the successful conclusion of the curse. When Wulumu saw the weapon, he knew what had transpired, and when he tried to swallow, he could not.

Wulumu would surely have died had it not been for the iron lung. Because of its respiratory support capability he became convinced that the white man's magic was greater than that of his tribe. He was right.

23. A Mother's Curses

Not all curse-deaths take place in primitive places. The following events for example, occurred in Oklahoma in 1960. The case involved a man who had been raised by a very domineering mother. When he decided to open a nightclub, she helped him finance it and then stayed on to assist with the management.

Some 14 years later, at age 38, he married and soon after decided to sell the club. His mother warned that if he sold out, "something dire will happen to you."

Two days after her threat the man, with no prior history of respiratory trouble of any kind, began to experience a mild attack of asthma. Nevertheless, he went ahead and sold the club. The day after the transaction he called his mother to tell her about it. She once again told him that "something will strike you." His asthmatic condition worsened at once, and he was rushed to the hospital.

A psychiatrist was able to help him see the link between his illness and his mother's warnings, and the asthmatic condition began to subside. Feeling better, the man began plans for another business, this time without his mother. Then one day, he called to tell her about it. She did not try to dissuade him but told him to expect more "dire results" if he persisted. Within an hour of that fateful phone call, he had another attack of asthma and died.

24. Deadly Love Spell of the Secret Statue

Because it casts a deadly love spell on men, a wooden statue of a beautiful woman is now hidden in the musty basement of the Naval Museum in La Spezia, Italy. The statue's shapely figure is revealingly clad in a brief garment from the era of classical Greece. "We believe it depicts the ancient goddess, Atalanta," said a naval officer recently. "We think it may have been the decorative prow on an ancient ship of the same name."

The crew of the Italian frigate, *Veloce,* discovered the statue floating in the middle of the Atlantic Ocean in 1864. "It will make a welcome decoration for the deck," said Captain Aristofane Caimmi. The statue was brought aboard, and crewmen immediately fell under the spell of the enchanting statue.

"Sailors gazed at 'her' for long periods of time," Captain Caimmi reported. "They seemed jealous when another man looked upon the statue. Quarrels developed, and fights broke out. I locked the statue in an empty cargo hold until we reached Genoa."

In 1879, the statue was moved from a warehouse in Genoa and placed in the Naval Museum at La Spezia. A guard at the museum claimed the statue had cast a "bewitching" spell on his mind. After talking about the statue's beauty hour after hour for many months, the disturbed guard committed suicide.

Erich Kurtz, a German soldier, was in charge of the museum during World War II. Also fascinated, he spent many hours staring at the statue of Atalanta. One afternoon, Kurtz stole the statue and hid it in his rented apartment. Now the statue of the beautiful goddess was his alone, he thought.

A short time later, the Wehrmacht military police were notified that the German soldier had not been at the museum for several days and made a routine call to their comrade's apartment. They found Kurtz dead at the foot of the statue. The soldier had committed suicide by firing a bullet into his head. The German Military Police official read the dead man's suicide note:

"Since no living woman can give me the life of my dreams, O Atalanta, I sacrifice my life to you!"

After the soldier's body was shipped home, the deadly statue of Atalanta was returned to the museum. "Put the cursed thing in the basement and keep it from the sight of men!" ordered a German Army officer. "Too many good men have fallen under her love spell."

The statue has been hidden since that time. Only her victims could recount the enchanting fascination of the lovely statue. And their lips are sealed – by death!

25. The *Flying Dutchman*

Of all the tales of the sea, none is ghostlier than that of the *Flying Dutchman.* The legend is based on an actual vessel, captained by a skilled but boastful seaman named Hendrik Vanderdecken, a Dutch East Indian who set sail from Amsterdam to Batavia, then a port in Dutch East India, in 1680. Though he was commissioned by a trading company to sail the company's boat and bring back a full load of cargo, Vanderdecken was certain he would bring back enough of his *own* loot to make himself rich as well.

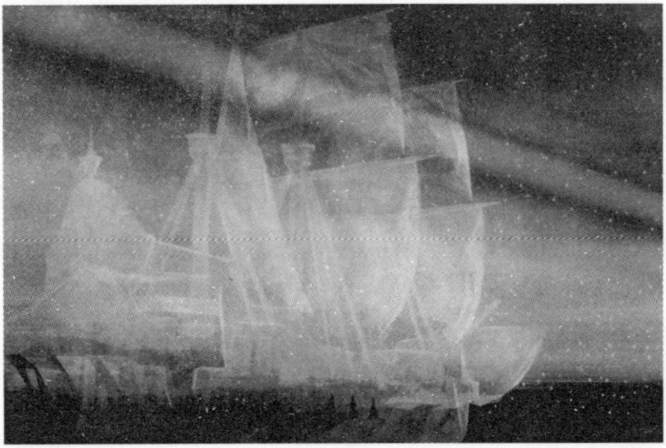

When Vanderdecken's ship was battered by a tropical storm, legend has it, he tried every manoeuvre he knew to advance the ship. The safe course would have been to wait out the storm, but prodded by a challenge from the devil in a dream one night, he decided to ignore the Lord's warnings and try to steer the ship around the Cape. It soon foundered, and the crew died. For his penance, it is said, Vanderdecken was cursed to sail his ship until Judgement Day.

An exciting and romantic legend it is, but witness after witness swears it is more. In 1835, the captain and crew of a British ship saw a phantom ship approaching through a heavy storm with all sails set, which suddenly disappeared as it came dangerously close. In 1881, sailors on the British ship *H.M.S. Bacchante* said a crew member fell from the rigging to his death the day after another midshipman saw the ghostly vision.

A more recent and highly acclaimed sighting of the *Dutchman* reportedly took place in March 1939, on Glencairn Beach in South Africa. The day following the sighting, a newspaper carried the story of dozens of bathers watching the ship, discussing details of the vision, and noting that it was full-sailed and moving steadily, despite the lack of any wind at the time.

Some scientists explained the group sighting as a mirage. But witnesses protested that it would have been difficult for them to envision a seventeenth-century sailing vessel in such detail, since most had never even seen one.

26. That Sinking Feeling

A Mississippi riverboat called the *Jo Daviess* sank after only three trips. Its engines were removed and installed on the steamboat *Reindeer*, and it sank, too. Salvaged once again, the engines were installed on the *Reindeer II*, which sank almost immediately. The engines were then used on the *Colonel Clay*, which sank after two trips. Next, the engines were installed on the *S.S. Monroe.* It was destroyed by fire. Salvaged for the fifth time, the engines were used in a gristmill, which burned to the ground!

27. Grave Warning

The Tomb of the Turkish conqueror Tamerlane (1336-1405) in Samarkand, East Uzbekistan, bore an inscription that read, "If I should be brought back to Earth, the greatest of all wars will engulf this land."

Soviet scientists, interested in studying historical burial practices, opened the tomb on June 22, 1941, at 5:00 a.m. and removed Tamerlane's mummified body. At the same moment, World War II broke out in Samarkand.

28. The Drummer of Cortachy Castle

Cortachy Castle, family seat of the Ogilvy Clan, is located north of Kirriemuir in Angus, Scotland. The Ogilvy ancestors became the first Earls of Angus after Scotland became a united country and their active participation in aiding William the Lion. It is reported that members of the Ogilvy Clan assisted King William who was ambushed and attacked while out hunting. As a reward for the assistance and their being staunch supporters of the monarchs, William the Lion awarded lands and titles to the Ogilvy Clan.

During the next three to four centuries, the Ogilvy Clan grew more and more powerful with each marriage that added more money and lands. The Ogilvy Clan became extremely powerful and influential and as is the case, they attracted enemies who resented their influence and power.

The Ogilvys were met with powerful enemies that attacked their strongholds and with the exception of Cortachy Castle, they were all brought down.

Earthly enemies were not enough for the Earl of Ogilvy. During the medieval times, it is said that a drummer and his drum were thrown from the highest turret of the highest tower. Some reports indicate that the young drummer was forcibly stuffed inside his drum and then tossed from the tower, surviving the fall long enough to curse the Ogilvy Clan. Whether his punishment was a result of a romantic liaison with the Earl's wife, the Countess of Airlie, or the drummer siding with the enemy, allowing them to enter the castle without beating out a warning, is unknown. One thing is for certain, he now beats his drum to warn the Ogilvy Clan. He warns them of an impending Ogilvy death.

For hundreds of years, the Ogilvy Clan has been haunted by a ghostly drumming that is heard by many witnesses. At Christmas time in 1844, a Miss Dalrymple was a guest at the castle. The evening Miss Dalrymple arrived she heard the beating of a drum as she dressed for dinner. During dinner she questioned her host about the identity of the drummer. The Lord and Lady Airlie paled at this question and told Miss Dalrymple that the last time the drummer was heard, the first Lady Airlie died shortly after. The next morning, Miss Dalrymple was treated to another serenade by the drummer. Spooked, Miss Dalrymple fled the castle immediately. Within six months, Lady Airlie died apparently by her own hand as there was a note left indicating that she knew the drummer was beating for her.

It was on August 19, 1849 that the drummer gave another serenade to a visiting Englishman. The Englishman was the guest of Lord Ogilvy, the heir to the Earldom of Airlie. The Englishman questioned several about the drumming only to be told they heard nothing. Before the Englishman could question Lord Ogilvy about the drummer, he was told that the 9th Earl of Airlie had become seriously ill requiring Lord Ogilvy's presence. The 9th Earl died the next day.

In 1900, the succeeding Earl died during the Boer War of 1900. No one near the Earl admits to having heard the beating of a drum. Since this Earl's death, no one else has reported hearing the mysterious beating of the drum. Could it be that the drummer felt he had had carried the curse out long enough?

29. The Jinxed Battleship

The famous ship *Scharnhorst* was dogged by bad luck from the moment of its launching. Few sailors doubt that there are such things as jinxed ships, unlucky from the day they were launched or before.

The 26,000-ton battleship *Scharnhorst* was such a ship. Launched in October 1936 as the pride of Nazi Germany, it should have had a long and successful career ahead; but from the beginning there were clear signs that all was not going well. Before the ship was half built it rolled over on the side, crushing 60 workmen to death and injuring over a 100 others. It took three months to raise it back into position. Workmen had to be drafted to complete the battleship because rumour had spread that it was jinxed. Later events seemed to substantiate the rumour.

When the time came for the important launching, Hitler, Goering, Himmler, and many other top Nazis were present.

Unfortunately, the *Scharnhorst* was not, having launched itself the night before. In the process, it ground up two barges as it hit the channel.

The exceptionally powerful long-range guns of the *Scharnhorst* were first used in the bombardment of Danzig in 1939, with unfortunate results. During the attack one of the guns exploded killing nine men, and the air supply to one of the gun turrets broke down, suffocating 12 gunners. A year later, during the bombardment of Oslo, the *Scharnhorst* was hit by more shells that all the rest of the German fleet combined. Fires broke out in over 30 places, and the ship had to be towed out of reach of the shore batteries. In making its way home for repairs, the battleship had to lie hidden from British bombers by day and move by night. At last it reached the safe haven of the Elbe river, but immediately ran into trouble again. Unknown to the *Scharnhorst*, the *SS Bremen* lay ahead. The ocean liner was one of the world's largest, and the glory of Germany. Too late the watch sounded an alarm, and seconds later the battleship rammed the prize liner. The *Bremen* sank and settled into the mud, where British planes bombed it to pieces.

After being repaired, the *Scharnhorst* was sent north in 1943 to cruise the coast of Norway and intercept convoys on their way to the Soviet Union. On the way there it passed and failed to notice a British patrol boat lying in the water with a disabled engine. When the battleship was safely over the horizon, the patrol boat radioed a warning. Several British warships steamed to the area and located the German battleship, but the *Scharnhorst* managed to escape the slower pursuers after a short exchange of fire. One of the pursuers caught a glimpse of the *Scharnhorst* from about 16,000 yards away, and the commander decided to fire a last shot. Knowing that the *Scharnhorst* would try to get out of the line of fire, he made a guess as to which direction to aim and gave the order to fire.

Living up to its jinx, the *Scharnhorst* turned directly into the path of the broadside from the British battleship. Flames shot up from the decks, and within minutes the German ship had plunged to the bottom of the icy sea with most of the crew. Only 36 survived out of a total of 1900. Years later it was discovered that two of the crew had succeeded in reaching a small rocky island where they made a windbreak from their raft. But the *Scharnhorst* jinx pursued them even there, for evidence showed that they were killed when their emergency oil heater exploded.

30. The Witch's Mark

The year was 1692, and 13 people had been hanged for witchcraft in Salem, Massachusetts. It was a matter of concern to Colonel Bucks, of Bucksport, Maine, that his own village should be just as vigilant in stamping out witches. He raised the question repeatedly at town hall meetings. Shortly his one-man crusade produced a victim.

There was a public accusation of a bent and withered old lady who looked every inch a witch. Historians disagree as to her name and age, but one of them calls her Comfort Ainsworth and is sure she was more than 90 years old.

Because of her obvious frailty, the old lady went on trial without torture or pricking with needles to find "the witch's mark". But the crowds that surged into the courtroom knew her guilt had been predetermined by Colonel Bucks himself, who sat within whispering distance of the magistrate. When witnesses took the stand against her, without exception they looked to Bucks for approval.

One woman said she had heard the old woman muttering something that sounded gibberish. But when she reached home and her ears started bleeding, she knew it had been a curse.

A man swore he'd seen a black-garbed figure ten feet tall – obviously the devil or one of his henchmen – standing in Comfort's doorway.

The jury quickly returned a verdict of guilty. Quoting the text, "Thou shalt not suffer a witch to live," the judge denounced Comfort Ainsworth and sentenced her to hang the next day.

No one was prepared for the scene that followed. Because she had not been permitted to testify in her own defence, people had assumed that the toothless old woman would remain mute.

Before the bailiffs could stop her, she got to her feet and pointed a bony finger at the colonel. "In all of my life," she screamed, "I have cursed no other being! But I am capable of laying a curse on you, sir, because you and your toadies have lied me to the gallows!

"Then mark you this, and mark it well – when you go to your grave, which will be soon, I pledge you I shall leave the print of my foot on your gravestone. And the print, Colonel Bucks, will be there forever so that the world can never forget this day!"

A bailiff clapped his palm to her mouth and carried her from the courtroom. But her words left the village uneasy, and there were few spectators when she was hanged next morning. Even Colonel Bucks failed to appear.

Three months later, he died from a "wasting disease", and the colonel's heirs found he had written a new instruction into his will. His headstone must be of the most flawless marble, "incapable of being stained or besmirched".

But in a few days the relatives were secretly approached by a terrified cemetery worker. He had found a woman's footprint in the marble, and no amount of sanding could remove it.

A new stonecutter was sworn to absolute secrecy. Working in the dead of night, he cut a marker that was an absolute replica of the first. The old stone was buried secretly and the new one raised.

Ten days later, the heirs saw crowds of frightened people moving in and out of the cemetery. Joining them, they found that the trick had failed. The shape of an old woman's narrow stockinged foot was clearly visible in the new stone.

Publicly deploring the phenomenon as an act of "graveyard vandalism" – an explanation that convinced no one – the heirs had a still more costly headstone hauled to the cemetery. It was raised with no attempt at secrecy. Incredibly, the print of Comfort's bony little foot soon began to take shape in the stone.

This time his discouraged heirs made no effort to replace the marker. Nearly three centuries later it stands over the grave of Colonel Bucks, the footprint still scarring its surface like a wound that will never heal.

31. A Dramatic Reversal

The active ill effects of a curse can immediately cease if the victim believes that he has been released from it. This indicates that the effects of curses, as recorded since ancient times, are psychosomatic.

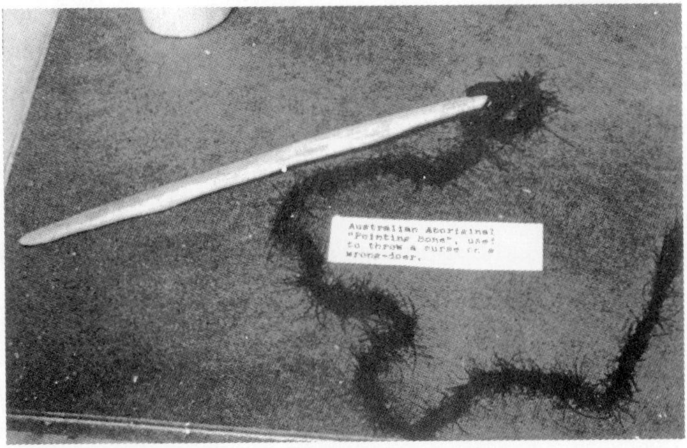

The following incident, which occurred in Australia around 1919, was later reported by Dr. S. M. Lambert during his association with the International Health Division of the Rockefeller Foundation. An example of a dramatic reversal, it makes the point:

At a Mission at Mona Mona in North Queensland were many native converts, but on the outskirts of the Mission was a group of non-converts including one Nebo, a famous witch doctor. The chief helper of the missionary was Rob, a native who had been converted. When Dr. Lambert arrived at the Mission he learned that Rob was in distress and that the missionary wanted him examined. Dr. Lambert made the examination, and found no fever, no complaint of pain, no symptoms or signs of disease. He was impressed, however, by the obvious indications that Rob was seriously ill and extremely weak. From the missionary he learned that Rob had had a bone pointed at him by Nebo and was convinced that in consequence he must die.

Thereupon Dr. Lambert and the missionary went for Nebo, threatened him sharply that his supply of food would be shut off if anything happened to Rob and that he and his people would be driven away from the Mission. At once Nebo agreed to go with them to see Rob. He leaned over Rob's bed and told the sick man that it was all a mistake, a mere joke – indeed, that he had not pointed a bone at him at all. The relief, Dr. Lambert testifies, was almost instantaneous; that evening Rob was back at work, quite happy again, and in full possession of his physical strength.

32. A Prophecy Self-fulfilled

On a Friday the 13th in 1946, a Georgia midwife was called upon to deliver three babies in the same area of the Okefenokee Swamp. For some malevolent reason, the woman put a curse on all three of the infant girls.

She said that one would die before she was 16 years of age, another would be dead before she reached 21, and the third would not live to see her 23rd birthday. The first two predictions were violently accurate. One girl, at 15, was in a fatal automobile accident. The second was killed by gunfire in a nightclub brawl the night before her 21st birthday.

Two years later, in 1969, the third young woman asked to enter a Baltimore hospital, declaring hysterically that she was doomed to die before her 23rd birthday, which was only three days away. Although there was apparently nothing wrong with her physically, she was obviously under great emotional stress and was admitted to the hospital for observation.

The next morning, just two days before the fateful date, the girl was found dead in her bed – the victim, evidently, of her belief in the power of the midwife's curse.

33. Gypsy Curse

For years, legend has it, the Epsom Derby was plagued by a curse, courtesy of a gypsy woman named Gypsy Lee. One year, it seems, the gypsy had predicted that a horse named Blew Gown would win the Derby, and she wrote her prediction down on a piece of paper for all to see. One of the owners at the track, however, haughtily pointed out that the horse was named Blue Gown, not spelled with a "w" at all. Bristling at the thought of looking foolish, Gypsy Lee issued a curse: No horse with a "w" in its name would win the Epsom Derby, she decreed, as long as she lived. And none ever did. But when Gypsy died in 1934, her mourning family bet all they could on Windsor Lad, and the horse won, paying seven-to-one.

34. Hands Off

In 1884, Walter Ingram returned to England with the mummified hand of an ancient Egyptian princess.

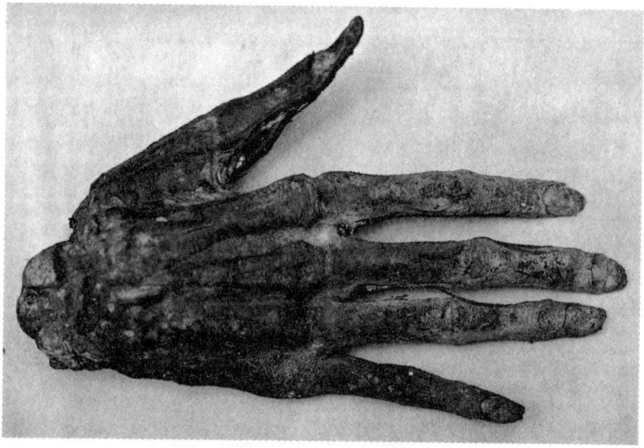

Clutched in the hand was a gold plaque that read, "Whoever takes me to a foreign land will die a violent death and his bones will never be found!" Four years later, Ingram was trampled to death by an elephant in Somaliland.

He was buried in a dry riverbed, but when an expedition was sent to bring Ingram's body back to England, they discovered that it had been washed away by a flood.

35. The Bell Witch

One of the most notorious American true ghost stories of all time is the story about the Bell Witch. The Bell Witch wasn't really a witch, but was a ghost or possibly even a demon. Tennesseans also sometimes refer to her as "Ol' Kate." This entity plagued the home of John Bell, a Clarksville, Tennessee cotton plantation owner of the early nineteenth century. John and his wife, had moved to Robertson County, Tennessee, from North Carolina. The woman whom John Bell bought his farm from, Kate Batts, claimed, to any and all who would listen, that she had been cheated by Bell, but no one paid her any attention and dismissed her accusations as mere senile ramblings. As a result, Kate Batts swore that she would get even with John Bell, even if she had to come back from the grave to do so. But whether the entity that stalked and terrorised the Bells for years was Kate Batts is unknown.

Though the problems did start around the time of Kate's death in 1817, that could be mere coincidence. It all began when John Bell was inspecting his rows of corn one day. He saw a bird that caused him alarm, for the creature had a face with human-like features. As it sat on the fencepost, staring at him, John shot at the bird, but missed. Unharmed, it flew away. Several days later, he encountered a snarling dog-like creature in the cornfield, and once again he shot at it, but this time the creature vanished before his very eyes.

The nine Bell children began seeing odd things as well. There were often sightings of creatures in the woods surrounding the farm and of a mysterious old woman sometimes wandering through the orchard. Then came the scratching and knocking sounds as if an animal were trying to burrow through the wall and get inside the house. Yet, when the Bells searched for the animal, they'd find nothing. Apparently the creature found some means of entrance for eventually the noises moved indoors, and often the family heard the loud sounds of wings flapping against the ceiling and dogs snarling and growling. These occurrences sounded more like a demonic manifestation rather than a typical haunting.

When word of the haunting got around no one could understand why such a foul entity would pester such a devout, religious family. Among those who wanted to aid the family in this crisis was General Andrew Jackson, who had masterminded the stirring victory at the Battle of New Orleans in 1812 and later became the seventh President of the United States. When he heard about how the ghost was tormenting the Bell family, he decided that a visit to John, his long time friend, was in order.

The trouble began as soon as his army wagon drew near, for his horses stood dead in their tracks, refusing to budge an inch even when the driver shouted and ferociously whipped them. The horses reportedly strained and pulled, attempting to move forward, but to no avail. It was as if some invisible force held them at bay.

When a voice echoed from somewhere in the darkness, "Go on, old General," the horses suddenly moved again. This convinced Jackson that there really was a terrible entity residing on the Bell property. "By the eternal, Boys!" he proclaimed to his men. "It is the witch!"

Nevertheless, Jackson's determination to learn more about the spectre didn't falter, and he and his entourage spent the night at the Bell home.

They were not disappointed! Betsy Bell screamed all night from the pinching and slapping she received from the ghost, and Jackson's covers were ripped off as quickly as he could put them back on. His entire party had similar experiences, being slapped, pinched, and poked by the ghost throughout the night. Unsurprisingly, by the time morning arrived, Jackson and his men were ready to scoot it out of there. Years later, after Jackson had taken office, he said: "I saw nothing, but I heard enough to convince me that I would rather fight the British than to deal with this torment they call the Bell Witch!"

Shortly after Jackson left the home, the supernatural activity in the Bell house intensified. The commotion rapidly worsened, and the knocking and rapping was incessant, so violent that it broke windows and shook walls. The roof of the place was pelted with what sounded like stones, but the projectiles were invisible. The family even heard heavy, invisible chains being dragged across the wooden floors.

Even worse were the attacks on the children who were chased from their beds by the fearful noise of scratching and gnawing. One night Richard Bell's hair was harshly grabbed by an invisible hand and yanked so hard that the boy was pulled from the comfort of his bed. This mode of attack became commonplace in the Bell household, and often Betsy was the victim.

When neighbour Jim Jones, a self-proclaimed exorcist heard about the haunting, he too went to the Bell Manor to see if he could help. After he performed an exorcism, the nightmare stopped for a little while, but all too soon, the spirit returned with a vengeance.

Again, it targeted the children, seeming to focus on Betsy, pulling little Betsy's hair and slapping her cheeks until they bled. Desperate, John and his wife decided to send the girl to a neighbour's home to spend the night, but the spirit followed her there and continued the attack.

Soon, the girl's health suffered from the abuse. As the months passed, she grew weaker and weaker, having fainting spells and difficulty breathing, the common effects of anxiety. It was around this time that the spirit started speaking, making its voice heard to all the members of the family in clear and understandable words. Maybe the entity had learned the language in the months it had haunted the family or maybe it had somehow summoned more power.

The spirit's desire to speak became more profound as the days passed, and it began to recite verses from the Bible, or it would utter ghastly threats. Often, it would laugh maniacally over its many foul actions.

Sceptics believed that it was 12-year-old Betsy herself who was responsible for the haunting, claiming that she was using sleight of hand, ventriloquism, and other tricks in order to attract attention. But this theory was quickly ruled out when a doctor came to stay overnight at the house. When the ghost starting spewing its horrible curses, he tightly covered Betsy's mouth...while the witch continued to cackle and taunt him. Betsy wasn't even in the room the night that William Porter, another neighbour who tried to help the family, stayed overnight.

As Porter lay sleeping, the covers were ripped from his body and wrapped into a ball. The man bolted upright, grabbing the ball of quilting, which he intended to toss into the fireplace, but the blanket was unusually heavy when he lifted it. While he stood there wondering what to do, a foul odour permeated the air, which became so strong that he was forced to flee the room. When he returned a few minutes later, the room was back to normal, and the ghost was gone.

Another neighbour, Frank Miles, a rather large, stout fellow, also wanted to help. He came to the Bell house with the full intention of volunteering to crush the witch with his powerful grip. As he spent the night at the Bell home, waiting for the opportunity to give the ghost the thrashing it deserved, the sheets were yanked off him. He quickly learned that he was no match for the strength of the spirit that struck him in the face and on the head. Later he claimed that they were some of the most powerful blows he had ever taken.

Even the Bells's slaves got a taste of the ghost's wickedness. It would periodically flog them.

The spirit, however, wasn't always wicked to everyone. The ghost actually appeared to like Mrs. Bell and would sometimes sing to her or do household chores to help her out. It seemed like the spirit's attack on Betsy and John remained the ghost's primary focus. And it almost seemed as if the ghost was jealous of Betsy and wanted to ruin her life.

Soon Betsy grew into a beautiful young woman and fell madly in love with a fine young schoolteacher, Joshua Gardner.

And though this match had pleased both families when the engagement was announced, the witch wasn't too happy about the turn of events! It promised Betsy that if she married Josh Gardner, she would never know a moment's peace and would be pinched and slapped until she bled. Terrified, Betsy broke-off the engagement.

It seemed that the witch was also determined to destroy Betsy's father.

John Bell's tongue would often become so thick and swollen that he couldn't eat or talk for hours at a time, and he developed an uncontrollable facial twitch, that was sometimes so severe that he'd be forced to stay in bed for days. In his last days as he tried to gain some strength by walking around his yard, the witch would wage an attack on him, knocking his shoes off his feet and knocking him to the ground.

His son, John Jr., would tie the shoes as tightly as possible, but that didn't deter the witch. In a fit of rage, it beat John Jr. so terribly that he required a doctor. The doctor prescribed a potion and left, and while John Jr. took to his bed, John Sr. became violently ill.

When the doctor returned, he called for the medicine bottle that he'd left for John Jr., but it was missing, and in its place was a thick, dark liquid that would defy analysis. As the Bells studied the liquid, the witch laughed frantically and said that it had placed it there.

On December 19, 1820, John's family feared the end was near when they found him in a stupor bordering on a coma. As they stood around the bed, the ghost informed them that it had fed John some poison, and it added, "Old Jack Bell will never get out of his bed again!"

The next morning, John was dead in his bed.

But the ghost wouldn't leave them alone. It even cursed and sang profane songs during John's funeral.

Strangely, however, after John was dead and Betsy's future happiness ruined, the witch announced to the family that it intended to leave, but would return in seven years.

As promised, it returned in 1828, making a racket like before, but its visit was uneventful, maybe because only Lucy and two of her sons remained in the house. The witch, however, wasn't yet finished with the Bell family, and it promised to return in 107 years, sometime in 1935, to pester the Bell descendants. Whether that promise was kept, no one knows, however, visitors claim that they can still feel a foul presence in the area that the witch once haunted.

36. Ecclescrieg House

Ecclescrieg House, in St. Cyrus, Aberdeenshire is another very spooky place. Bram Stoker used to spend his holidays at nearby Cruden Bay, and it is said that he used the old house as inspiration for Count Dracula's castle.

It is supposedly haunted due to a curse that was placed on the original owners, the Forsyth-Grant family.

It all started when Osbert Clare Forsyth-Grant, who lived from 1880 to 1911, joined the Navy against the wishes of his father. Supposedly, he sailed from Montrose to command a whaling ship whose crew was composed of Scots and Eskimos. Something happened between Osbert and the Eskimos, no one seems to know what, but they put a curse on him and his family. Not long afterward his ship, the *Seduisante* was wrecked in a storm and went missing. It seems there was a mutiny and killing on board, but no one knows what happened for sure, because only a few Eskimos lived to tell about it.

But Grant's body was never found. It is said that his father never quite recovered from the incident and continually stood on the terrace, staring into some binoculars at the sea, and hoping his son would return. The old man is still seen walking the grounds today, waiting for a son that will never return.

37. Unlucky Plane

The jinx on the Lockheed Constellation airliner AHEM-4 began the day in July 1945 when a mechanic walked into one of the plane's propellers and was killed. Precisely one year later, on July 9, 1946, Captain Arthur Lewis died at the controls while the plane was over the Atlantic Ocean. Precisely one

more year later, on July 9, 1947, a newly installed engine burst into flames shortly after takeoff. The captain, Robert Norman, succeeded in putting out the flames with a fire extinguisher, but then found that the plane lacked enough power to climb above the roof of an apartment building directly in their path. Norman switched on the takeoff power and just managed to climb out of danger, but when he tried to ease the power off again, the controls remained jammed. He and his copilot finally wrestled the controls back by sheer force, and landed without further mishap.

July 1948 passed uneventfully. But on July 10, 1949, the airliner crashed near Chicago, killing everyone on board including Captain Robert Norman. The AHEM-4's jinx was his bad luck.

38. The Skulls of Calgarth

Wealthy Myles Phillipson owned huge tracts of the picturesque English Lake District countryside around Windermere, during the 16th century. But he was never satisfied with the extent of his empire, always restlessly seeking new acres to add to his estates. He eyed the small farm of Kraster and Dorothy Cook, which overlooked the lake. And he decided that their humble plot of land would be the ideal site for the new luxurious mansion he planned.

The farm was all the Cooks had in the world, and they were not prepared to sell when Phillipson made his offer. He was not a man to take 'no' for an answer. He invited the poor couple to share Christmas dinner with him and his family. The Cooks were awed by the foods and wines, and overjoyed when the landowner said they could keep a golden bowl they admired.

Next morning, soldiers hammered at the door of their home, and arrested them. For a week they were held in separate cells, with no idea why they were being imprisoned. Only when they arrived in court did they learn of their "crime" – stealing a golden bowl from Myles Phillipson.

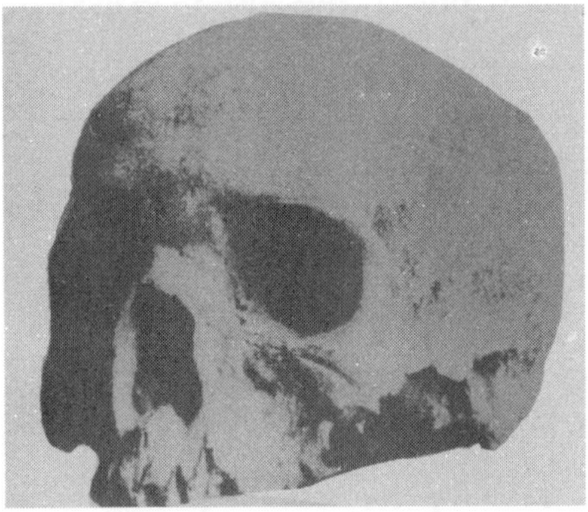

The verdict was a foregone conclusion, because the magistrate hearing the case was Phillipson himself. When he sentenced them both to death, Dorothy Cook cried out: "Look out for yourself, you will never prosper. The time will come when you own no land. You will never be rid of us......."

Phillipson was not worried by the threats. The couple were hustled to the gallows, and strung up to die.

Within days, Phillipson had acquired their land and started work on his magnificent new home, called Calgarth Hall. When it was finished, he held a lavish Christmas feast to celebrate. Friends and neighbours joined him round the table, making merry with no expense spared.

Then a terrifying scream sent them rushing upstairs, swords at the ready.

Phillipson's wife stood halfway up the staircase, shuddering as she stared transfixed at a hideous sight on the bannister – two grinning skulls. The landowner seized them, threw them into the courtyard, and swore revenge on whoever had perpetrated the tasteless joke.

But his threats failed to put the minds of his guests at rest. Several shuffled off to bed early – only to be woken in the small hours by more screams. The skulls were back on the stairs.

Over the next few days, Phillipson tried everything he knew to get rid of them. But each time they were thrown outside or buried, the skulls returned to haunt the home.

Christmas was ruined. And as the news spread, so was Phillipson. His business declined, his riches dwindled. When he died, a broken man, his beautiful home rang all night with the demonic laughter of the skulls.

The two gruesome relics continued to visit the hall, giving the landowner's heirs no rest. They appeared each Christmas Day, and on the anniversary of the Cooks's execution. Only when the family became too poor to maintain Calgarth, and were forced to sell it, did the skulls leave the building in peace.

39. Possessed!

Terry Palmer set out to find the resting place of the last witch in England to be burned at the stake. But his quest took him along an unnerving path – with his own body taken over by the witch he sought.

The spirit said she would be with Terry for all time, no matter where he went.

England's last witch, whose name was Elsa, was tortured and burned to death on the old village green of Dedham, Essex, in 1763. More than 200 years later, Terry set out to find her burial place. But everywhere he went, inexplicable happenings took place.

He once visited a former convent where a terrier dog ran out to greet him, barking and wagging its tail. Then it ran back to its master, before bounding back – right past Terry. It was barking and leaping at an empty space.

A few days later in a shop, another dog barked twice at Terry.........and then twice at the empty space behind him.

The extraordinary tale of Terry, a good, book publisher, began when he went to a seance on his witch-hunting trail. There, says Terry, Elsa herself took over his body and joined in the ghost hunt.

Shortly afterwards, his father became possessed by evil spirits, and a fire broke out in his factory causing thousands of pounds of damage.

Terry claimed to have found Elsa's grave, near a hotel not far from the tiny village where she was executed. He stood on the spot and felt a tingling sensation from the back of his head to the middle of his spine. But when he and a friend dug down they found nothing.

Terry's story was told in the hotel and was treated with scepticism – until one day when a barman was having lunch while keeping an eye on the empty bar through a mirror. He saw a woman standing in the room and went to serve her. But the bar was empty, and all the doors were locked.

40. The Curse of Garra

An oasis in the Libyan desert, in North Africa, was cursed more than three centuries ago and the malediction still blights the life of its inhabitants – to an unbelievable degree. The name of the oasis is Garra, located about 75 miles west of Siwa. More than 300 years ago, the men of Garra committed an unpardonable act of sacrilege by waylaying and robbing a caravan of Mecca-bound pilgrims. The leader of the caravan, a venerable old man named Abdel Sayed, pronounced an imprecation upon Garra – to the effect that there should never be more than forty men alive at the same time. In this nuclear

era it is difficult to give credence to the efficacy of a curse uttered so long ago. Nevertheless, it is a fact that the blight has been in full and terrifying effect to the present day. No sooner does a boy grow into man-hood than an older man is invariably stricken and dies. In World War I, an Australian military detachment, numbering eighteen men, was temporarily stationed in Garra. The Aussies had hardly arrived when an epidemic struck the population and eighteen deaths occurred – to restore the balance. The sheik of Garra thereupon urgently petitioned the Australian command to withdraw the detachment without any replacements. The Army command, apprised of the strange circumstances, complied at once.

41. The Hoodoo Ship - the *Hinemoa*

The *Hinemoa*, a 2,000-ton steel bark built in Scotland in 1890 for the frozen mutton trade from New Zealand, suffered from ill luck during her entire existence. On her maiden voyage to New Zealand in 1892 four of her apprentices died of typhoid. Her first captain became insane, her second, a criminal. Her third master was declared a hopeless alcoholic, her fourth was found dead in his cabin with a revolver at his side. Her fifth skipper blew his brains out. The ship capsized on her sixth voyage. She was righted again. Her seventh crossing was marred by the loss of two sailors washed overboard. She finally drifted ashore – a total wreck off Lorne Jetty – in 1908.

Superstitious sailors whispered the secret of the curse that seemed to dog the *Hinemoa's* steps. On her maiden voyage she took aboard as ballast a load of rubble from an old London graveyard. She was a marked jinx from then on.

42. U-Boat 65

Almost two years into the Great War, the battlefields of France and Belgium were literally running red with blood. Hundreds of thousands of young men were dying, an entire generation consigned to the mud and mayhem of trench warfare along the Western Front. The conflagration was so evenly matched that victories were measured in mere yards.

Neither side could muster the reserves for that one decisive thrust to punch through the other's defences, and the war developed into a grotesque stalemate – except that in this case, the pawns were the young men of England, Germany and France.

The only breakthrough in the war, it seemed, might come at sea where, by the summer of 1916, the Kaiser's navy, led by the wolf packs of U-boat submarines, was beginning to take a heavy toll on British shipping. Hundreds of thousands of tons were consigned to the bottom of the seas by the fast-moving U-boats. Particularly hard hit was the British merchant fleet, which carried supplies vital to the war effort in Europe.

The Kaiser and his navy warlords were convinced that this was the way to break the back of the British bulldog and so, with the war two years old, Germany was devoting much of its total war effort to producing more and more submarines to press the attack. That year, among the many U-boats which came down the assembly line ready for British blood was *UB65*, which would go down in naval lore as the host to at least one ghost, and the scene of many disturbing and tragic occurrences. Indeed, *UB65* became so infamous, that even as the war raged on, its panic-stricken crew grew increasingly reluctant to sail on her.

Even before she was launched, the 'Iron Coffin' as she became known, seemed to attract disaster. She was built to join a fleet of submarines prowling off the Flemish coastline, gorging on the slow, heavily laden ships crossing back and forward across the English Channel. But it seemed that everything that could go wrong during construction, did.

Not even seven days into her construction, as the hull was being laid, the first tragedy struck. As workers poured over the site, a giant girder hovering overhead on chains suddenly broke free, plunging into the hull. A hapless worker was horribly crushed under its massive weight, and lay there in agony for over an hour while frantic mates tried to rescue him. Tragically, he died just as the huge weight was finally lifted off him. An inquiry into the accident found there had been no faults in the chains used to hoist the girder, and officials were mystified as to what could have caused it to snap free. Less than two months later, there was a second, more alarming tragedy. Three engineers who were assigned to the U-boat's engine room to test the submarine's dry cell batteries, were overcome by deadly chloride fumes. They died before anyone could rescue them and drag them into the fresh air. No one ever determined why the batteries ever leaked the toxic fumes.

Thankfully, there were no more mysterious incidents during the remaining construction and shortly afterwards *UB65* set sail for sea trials. But whatever dogged the boat seemed to follow it out of port because it quickly ran into a fierce Channel storm, and one hapless sailor was washed overboard to his death when the vessel came up to test her stability on the surface during rough seas.

After the man went overboard, the captain ordered the U-boat to dive. As she did, a ballast tank sprang a leak, flooding the dry-cell batteries in sea water and filling the engine room with the same deadly gas that had already claimed three lives while the boat was still on the slipway. After 12 nerve-racking hours the crew final managed to get the ship to surface, where they flung open the hatches and breathed clean air. Amazingly, no one was killed and the bedevilled craft limped back to Germany for repairs.

After several days, the U-boat was again readied for sea and her first on-line patrol. But as a battery of torpedoes was being placed on board, a warhead suddenly exploded, killing the second officer and badly wounding several others. Yet again, an inquiry was conducted, but no explanation for the explosion was ever found. In the meantime, the second officer was buried, and another round of repairs made to the jinxed vessel. Her jittery crew, already worried about the U-boat's growing reputation for being accursed, were given a few days' much-needed shore leave to calm their shattered nerves before setting out on their first active patrol.

Yet just moments before she was set to leave port, another bizarre incident occurred – this time, a panicked sailor swore he had seen the apparition of the dead second officer. *"Herr Kapitan!"* he blurted. *"The dead officer is on board!"* The captain, of course, refused to take the report seriously, believing the sailor had had too much to drink during his shore leave. However, even the stoic skipper was a little taken aback when a second member of his crew also claimed to have seen the ghost of the second officer coming casually up the gangplank! The seaman was sobbing from fear when he told the captain that the apparition had walked aboard, strolled up to the bow, then looked out at the inviting sea. He then vanished into thin air.

That two crew members had reported seeing the dead officer gave the captain some reason for pause, but nevertheless he knew his duty lay at sea and in sinking British ships. *UB65* had some early successes on its maiden voyage, sinking three Allied merchant ships in quick succession. However, the rumours of the unwanted ghost had spread through the crew like wildfire, and their celebration over any direct hits was tempered by their belief that their vessel was haunted.

Indeed, there was almost full-scale panic after *UB65* recorded its second kill, when startled sailors in the engine room saw the dead officer observing the instrument panel as he had done in the trial voyage. By the time the submarine returned to base, rumours of its ghostly visitor were already spreading throughout the entire U-boat armada. The captain did his best to dispel the talk, claiming it was all poppycock, fearing that the ghost tales would only further erode the morale of the 34-man crew. But in their hearts, the men of *UB65* knew something was terribly amiss with their craft.

Then in January 1918, as the war dragged ever closer to its inevitable conclusion, even the captain could no longer dismiss the sightings as the rantings of some foolhardy seamen – for he, too, saw the apparition! It came as the U-boat was prowling in the Channel off Portland Bill. Because the weather was so foul and the seas extremely rough, the captain ordered the craft to surface. After breaking the surface, a lookout stationed on the starboard side was scanning the stormy horizon. He turned to look to port, when suddenly he spotted an officer standing on the deck, which heaved under the growing fury of the waves. At first, the crew man thought the officer foolhardy for taking such a risk, but then realised that all the hatches were still battened down. Bar the one from which he himself had climbed onto the deck. He knew no one could have come up through there without him immediately spotting him.

Suddenly, the crew man got a full look at the officer – and his face went white as the blood drained from it. There standing in front of him was the second officer, who had been buried with full honours back at home base. When he finally summoned the courage to move, the terrified seaman screamed to his shipmates that the ghost was on the boat. Below deck, the crew were close to all-out panic, and the captain had to act immediately lest a hysterical sailor put all their lives in jeopardy. He raced up the ladder, fully expecting to see nothing save a panicked crew man, when he, too, saw his dead comrade, his face a grotesque distortion. Seconds later, the ghost vanished, as if blown into the raging swell by the strong winds.

By the time the U-boat returned to port, navy authorities were already waiting. They were determined to get to the bottom of the mystery, fearing that the morale of the crew was so low that another disaster was just waiting to happen. With intense secrecy, each and every man assigned to *UB65* was interviewed by a panel of high-ranking officers.

The reader must remember that U-boat crews were among the most reliable and hardiest in the navy. They were subjected to long periods of confinement deep below the ocean surface, and had to withstand hours of nerve-racking pursuit by Allied destroyers. It was a fact that a submariner had only a 50-50 chance of ever returning from his mission, and that on a man-for-man basis, the U-boat force suffered the highest casualties of the war. So when these brave, innately fearless men told navy officials that they were terrified of returning to their craft because of ghosts, then their story could not simply be dismissed as irrational rantings. And it wasn't. Although the Kaiser's sea lords could never admit to having a haunted ship – one could imagine the widespread effect on morale that would have on their other crews – they found the stories about the ghost of the dead second officer too convincing to simply laugh off or dismiss as the talk of overwrought sailors. Instead, they decided to break up the crew of *UB65,* sending some to other submarines and others to destroyers.

But that still left the problem of what to do with the vessel itself. Eventually, the U-boat was decommissioned at the port of Bruges, in Belgium, and a Lutheran pastor was asked to perform the ancient Christian rite of exorcism! In surely what must be one of the most incredible wartime scenes ever, a Belgian civilian was taken on board while German officers watched with a mixture of fascination and dread. Once the exorcism was completed, everyone breathed a sigh of relief.

A new crew and captain were assigned to the 'cleansed' ship, and it was business as usual for the next few weeks. The new skipper, a stern disciplinarian who scoffed at the stories of dead men walking the ship, warned his crew that he would not tolerate any renewed tales of ghosts or goblins. For the next two missions, it appeared as if everything was back to normal. There had been no sightings and no inexplicable accidents. But in May 1918, the ghost appeared again.

During the long voyage, in which *UB65* was ordered to patrol the sea lanes off the Spanish coast as well as the English Channel, the dead officer was seen no fewer than three times. One of those who saw the ghost was the petty officer, who swore to God that he saw the man walk though a solid iron bulkhead and pass into the engine room! Another man, a torpedo handler, claimed the ghost visited him several times at night. The terrified soul became so disoriented that when the submarine surfaced to recharge its batteries, he leaped off the deck to his death in the seas.

On its final voyage – during July 1918, just four months before the Armistice was signed and peace returned to a ravaged Europe – *UB65* was spotted by an American submarine resting like a sitting duck on the surface. No one knows why. It was July 10. The American sailors, who couldn't believe their good fortune, quickly armed their torpedoes and prepared to fire. But just before they did, *UB65* suddenly exploded, sending the remains of metal and men spewing out over a wide range of ocean.

Within seconds, all that remained of the submarine and her crew was a heavy oil slick and scattered debris. No one aboard the American submarine ever gave the order to fire, and the crew swears no one launched a torpedo. What happened? To this day, no one knows. But it seemed a fitting, if bloody, end to the story of the haunted ship, which took its most enigmatic secret with it to its watery grave.

43. The Winchester Mystery House

The Winchester Mansion is located in San Jose, California, America. Tours are given on a daily basis, and on Halloween and every Friday the 13th there are torchlight tours. The Mansion has a very interesting history.

Sarah Winchester was once a prominent member of the Boston elite society.

After the deaths of her only child, a girl, and Sarah's husband who was the son and heir of the man who produced the Winchester repeating rifles, Sarah thought the reason her child and husband had died was because the spirits of everyone killed by the Winchester rifle had taken them and placed a curse on the Winchesters. The only way to appease the spirits was to build a mansion and keep building it forever. Thus began a 38-year quest by Sarah Winchester to not only appease the spirits but confuse them as well so they couldn't find her.

The wealthy Mrs. Winchester at the age of 44 travelled alone to San Jose, California, to build a mansion and kept the construction going for the next 38 years until her death. The house at one time rose 7 storeys and contained a maze of rooms, hallways, staircases and doors. She named her mystery house Llanda Villa. It was a 160-room mansion although Sarah closed off the front 30 rooms. She boarded them up after an earthquake in 1906. She took the earthquake as a sign that the spirits were unhappy with the way the construction was going. However, estimates point to over 600 rooms built and demolished over a 38-year time frame.

One feature of the Mansion was a bell tower, where the bell was rung every night at about midnight to summon the spirits. Sarah would then ask the good spirits how they wanted the mansion constructed. The bell would again ring out at 2 a.m. to signal the spirits that it was time to leave.

Sarah would emerge from the seance room with new plans for the construction workers. She claimed the good spirits gave her the plans to help her confuse the bad spirits so they couldn't get to her.

Many psychics have spent the night at the Winchester Mansion hoping to contact the spirits that reside there. They were not disappointed.

Experiences include organ music being heard in the Blue Room where Sarah died. In Sarah's bedroom cold spots are felt and red balls of light are seen that seem to explode and fade. Apparitions of a couple lingering in the corner of the bedroom clothed in servants garb dating to the early 20th century. The sense of being watched is also felt in many parts of the house.

During one seance a psychic appeared to age dramatically and take on the physical appearance of Sarah. Although most people who have felt Sarah have said she is a kind and gentle spirit.

A caretaker who worked at the house for several years said he heard breathing in one room, and once had followed the sound of footsteps to the doorway of Sarah's bedroom.

Both instances he was alone. Another worker in the house claimed to have heard his name whispered. While still others have sensed being watched, hearing footsteps, and perhaps the strangest of all, the smell of chicken soup coming from the front kitchen that had not been in use for several years.

Apparitions of Sarah have been seen and photographed, as well as a man in overalls.

There were many episodes of lights turning off and on by themselves when the house is empty and locked up for the night. Also, a room in the house was flooded, every item in the room was soaked. Upon further inspection the floor, the ceiling and the walls of the room were completely dry.

Although Sarah Winchester lived her life in solitude and reclusive for the last 38 years of her life, it would seem she enjoys putting on a show for the workers and tour groups who visit her unique home now.

44. Death Car

There are records of cars that seem to have brought disaster to their owners. One example is the car in which the Archduke Franz Ferdinand, heir to the dual monarchy of Austria-Hungary, and his wife were assassinated at Sarajevo in July 1947 – a murder that precipitated the outbreak of World War I. Shortly after the start of the war, General Potiorek of the Austrian army came into possession of the car. A few weeks later he suffered a catastrophic defeat against the Serbians at Valjevo, and was sent back to Vienna in disgrace. He could not endure the shame of this and died insane.

The next owner of the car was an Austrian captain who had been on Potiorek's staff. Only nine days after taking over the car, he struck and killed two peasants, then swerved into a tree and broke his neck.

At the end of the war, the Governor of Yugoslavia became the owner of the car. After four accidents in four months – one of which caused him to lose an arm – he had had enough, and sold the car to a doctor. Six months later the car was found upside down in a ditch. The doctor had been crushed to death inside it. The car was next sold to a wealthy jeweller who committed suicide only a year later. After a brief spell in the hands of another doctor, who seems to have been all too anxious to get rid of it, the car was sold to a Swiss racing driver. He was killed in a race in the Italian Alps when the car threw him over a wall. The next owner was a Serbian farmer. Having stalled the car one morning, he persuaded a passing motorist to give him a tow – and became the car's tenth victim in a bizarre accident. Because he forgot to turn off the ignition, the car started up, smashed the horse and cart, and overturned on a bend. The car's final owner was Tibor Hirshfeld, a garage owner. Returning from a wedding with six friends one day, Hirshfeld tried to overtake another car at high speed. He crashed and was killed along with four of his companions. The car was then taken to a Vienna museum, where it has been ever since.

45. The Bloodstone Ring

Gale force winds lashed the tiny English village of Willisham, ripping slates from the roofs and tearing limbs from trees. A huge old oak shuddered before the onslaught and then, caught by one mighty gust, toppled, its roots tearing at the earth beneath.

Villagers who rushed to the spot to see if anyone was hurt stopped in horror as they gazed between the gnarled roots. There lay some human remains.

Police Constable Klug, the only bobby in the East Anglian community, was called and he ordered that the body be taken from its strange grave. One of the dismembered hands had a ring on one finger. Acting on a hunch, the grim-faced constable carried the hand to Ellen Grey, sister of a girl who had vanished mysteriously 18 years before, in 1873. Ellen screamed and then hugged the ghastly relic to her breast.

"It's Mary's," she sobbed. "The bloodstone ring was my wedding gift. She was born in March, and it was her birthstone."

Klug understood. Though the case was before his time, it was so well known in the area it had been the subject of a popular ballad.

On her 18th birthday, Mary Grey had married Basil Osborne. She had written a letter to John Bodneys, her sweetheart since childhood, asking for his forgiveness.

An hour before the groom was to take her away on the honeymoon, Mary told her sister she wanted to spend a little time alone in the upstairs room they had shared. When Osborne arrived with the carriage, she still hadn't come down. Frightened, they forced their way into the locked bedroom, but found no trace of the bride.

One window opened onto a balcony where a flight of steps led to an enclosed garden. But the garden, too, was empty.

The abandoned bridegroom died a month later. The villagers blamed a broken heart.

Now, 18 years later, the village knew what had become of Mary – for the skeleton had a broken neck! Ellen refused to give up her murdered sister's hand. It had been brought to her for a purpose, she said. That purpose must be fulfilled.

Dying, she left a bizarre provision in her will. Her housekeeper Maggie Williams was to have her estate, but must display the hand in some public place "where it may some day confront the murderer."

Maggie opened what became the finest pub in Willisham and gave the hand a place of honour on one wall. Enclosed in glass against a black velvet background, the bony ringed fingers claimed the attention of everyone.

After the shock of the exhibit had worn away, the tale of Mary's murder was a frequent topic of conversation. On a dismal March night in 1895, a stranger sat listening to scraps of the talk.

"Must have been just such a night as this that the wind ripped out that old oak tree," said the publican.

The stranger, a brooding man with a ravaged face, looked up from his glass. "I don't understand. What oak tree?" he asked.

"Have a look at the case on the wall and then we'll tell you the story," the barman told him.

Moments later, the stranger was screaming. He sagged against the wall, blood dripping from his fingers. An older man at the bar recognised him as Mary's missing former sweetheart John Bodneys.

When Constable Klug arrived, the bleeding man confessed to the murder of Mary Grey. In a frenzy of jealousy, he had found the bride alone in her room. Muffling her cries, he carried her from the house.

Bodneys insisted that he had not meant to kill her. But when they reached the big oak tree, she was struggling so hard he had broken her neck.

He left her in a shallow grave under the oak and tried to put Willisham behind him forever. But there had never been a moment of peace since the crime, and inevitably he had been compelled to return.

Committed to the local jail to await trial, he died "of no known disease" before his trial could be held. The authorities dismissed the old wives' tale that a murderer's hands sometimes drip blood when he faces the proof of his crime. But the people of the village knew what they had seen.

They buried Mary Grey's hand with the rest of her skeleton – and then ceremoniously burned the shirt smeared by John Bodneys' bloody fingers the day he came face to face with his guilt.

46. The Relentless *Kurdaitcha*

In 1953 an Aborigine named Kinjika was flown from his native Arnhem Land in Australia's Northern Territory to a hospital in Darwin, the territorial capital. He had not been injured or poisoned, was not suffering from any known disease, but he was dying. Kinjika survived for four days in great pain after entering the hospital, and on the fifth day he died, the victim of bone pointing, a method of execution – or murder – that leaves no trace and almost never fails.

The dead man had been a member of the Mailli tribe and had broken one of its laws governing incestuous relationships. Following this he had been summoned before a tribal council, had refused to attend, and in his absence had been sentenced to death.

Kinjika then fled his homeland, and the tribal executioner, the *mulunguwa,* made and ritually "loaded" the killing-bone, or *kundela.*

The bone used may be human, kangaroo, or emu, or it may be fashioned from wood. The design varies from tribe to tribe. Most are from six to nine inches long, pointed at one end, and shaved to a smooth roundness. At the other end a braid of hair is attached through a hole or with a resinous gum derived from the spinifex bush. To be effective, the *kundela* must be charged with powerful psychic energy, in a complex ritual that must be performed faultlessly. The process is kept secret from women and all who are not members of the tribe. If the condemned man has fled from his village, the loaded bone is given to the *kurdaitcha,* the tribe's ritual killers.

The *kurdaitcha* take their name from the special slippers they wear when hunting a condemned man. These are woven from cockatoo feathers and human hair and leave virtually no footprints. The hunters clothe themselves with kangaroo hair, which they stick to their skin after first coating themselves with human blood, and they don masks of emu feathers. Usually operating in two's or three's, they are relentless and will pursue their quarry for years, if necessary.

When the hunters finally corner their man, they approach to within 15 feet or so, and one *kurdaitcha,* or "hit man," dropping to his knee, holds the bone in his fist and points it like a pistol. At this instant, the condemned man is said to be frozen with fear. The *kurdaitcha* thrusts the bone towards him and utters a brief piercing chant. He and his fellow hunters then withdraw, leaving the pointed man to his own devices. When they return to their village, the *kundela* is ceremonially burned.

The condemned man may live for several more days or weeks. But convinced of the *kundela's* fatal power, his relatives and members of any other tribe he may meet (who will certainly have heard that he has been pointed) treat him as though he were already dead.

The ritual loading of the *kundela* creates a psychic counterpart of the bone – a "spear of thought," as it has been described – which pierces the condemned man when the bone is pointed at him. Once he has been wounded, the victim's death is certain, as though an actual spear had been thrust through him.

47. Devil's Marbles

In 1980, a strange Aborigine curse was re-invoked in the Australian outback when a boulder was removed from a religious site. The boulder formed part of the so-called Devil's Marbles, which the Aborigines said had been cursed by their forefathers from time immemorial.

When the boulder was removed to a national park, Aborigine leader Mick Taylor warned that sickness and death would follow. Several Aborigine children fell ill and Taylor himself caught meningitis. An urgent meeting of councillors in the town of Tennant Creek had the stone returned and the children completely recovered. But it was too late for poor Mick Taylor.

48. Roche Castle

Roche Castle, in Pembrokeshire, is purported to be another very haunted castle. It has been associated with supernatural happenings since the thirteenth century. It is said that the owner, Adam de la Roche, was cursed by a witch that an adder would bite him and kill him. Terrified of the tale, Roche built the castle high upon a rock where there was no moorland or undergrowth to attract the creatures. Nevertheless, even safely hidden in his mighty fortress, Roche remained horrified of the prophecy and became a recluse behind the thick walls.

Yet amazingly, a snake did manage to find it's way into Roche's castle.

On a cold winter night, a servant had carried in a bundle of twigs for the great hall fire, and apparently an adder emerged from the wood late that night, to bite the sleeping nobleman on the leg.

Roche was discovered dead the next morning.

Roche Castle is also haunted by the ghost of Lucy Walters, who was the mistress of King Charles II. Lucy, who was supposedly a beautiful woman, met the king in Holland when she was on vacation with her lover, Colonel Robert Sydney.

She and Charles instantly felt some kind of chemistry for each other, and she soon became the mother of Charles' son, the Duke of Monmouth. Unfortunately, the king tired of Lucy. He put his favourite bastard son under the care of his wife, but, sadly, he spurned Lucy. As a result, she died from poverty at only twenty-eight years old.

Her ghost, cloaked in white, is said to be seen walking about Roche Castle, even floating through shut and locked doors. It is said that she even awakens sleepers at night.

49. The Death of James Dean

Everyone knows that James Dean was killed in his expensive Porsche 550 Spyder. His fans were devastated to hear the news about the two car crashes that occurred on September 30, 1955. When his blockbuster hit *Rebel Without A Cause* opened a month later, theatres across the nation were packed with teary-eyed, heart-broken audiences. Everyone was in shock that someone so young and vital would be snatched away so unexpectedly.

But could there be something more sinister involved in Dean's death than an everyday tragedy? There are many strange occurrences surrounding Dean's death, including a jinxed Porsche Spyder, a possible curse, and black magic. There may have even been a malevolent force in the car with him on the fateful evening of his death.

A lot of people, including historians and parapsychologists, would swear that something supernatural was at work...that some unseen entity or black magic is responsible for Dean's death and the other strange occurrences afterwards. Yet, if evil was at work, it appears that some other force attempted to intervene and warn him. Amazingly, on the day the fatal accident occurred, Dean received no fewer than four warnings about his reckless driving speed. But in reviewing the events of the day of the tragedy, it appears that Dean had no idea that the day would be his last.

September 30 was pretty much an ordinary day for Dean. Early that morning he got dressed as usual, wearing his favourite red jacket from *Rebel Without A Cause*. Then he drove to Competition Motors where his mechanic, Rolf Wütherich, thoroughly inspected the Spyder for the upcoming race that Dean would be participating in. They headed for Salinas with *Life* photographer, Sandy Roth and stuntman, Bill Hickman, who drove in a separate vehicle.

When the four stopped at a roadside restaurant, Hickman warned Dean, who was nonchalantly drinking a cold glass of milk, not to drive too fast. Was this some kind of portend about the tragedy to come? Maybe and maybe not. It's possible that Hickman was simply perturbed that the station wagon that he and Sandy were in just couldn't keep up with the fast Porsche Spyder, and Roth wanted to get some pictures of the beloved celebrity on the road.

Though two weeks earlier Dean had told TV viewers in a National Safety Council commercial "remember, drive safely, the life you might save might be mine," he nevertheless had a propensity for speeding. Everyone knew that he drove fast both on and off the track. When he started on location for the George Stevens epic *Giant*, he was forbidden by contract to race, but the ultimatum didn't end his fascination with fast cars.

When the shooting in Texas ended, he immediately

purchased the flashy Porsche Spyder, that had the number "130" painted in red on each door, and "Little Bastard" painted on the back.

Was it possible that Hickman had bad vibes when he saw the gleaming silver car, or was he somehow sensing what was to come? If he did harbour such feelings, he didn't breathe a word about it that day, and soon, the group was back on the road, heading north on Highway 99, now Highway 5. Despite Hickman's request, Dean quickly accelerated up to 68 m/ph. on Grapevine Road, breaking the speed limit.

Still, Dean would get another warning about his driving speed when, at around 3:30, Police officer Otie V. Hunter pursued the vehicle and made Dean pull over. The ticket failed to dissuade the reckless young man, however, because immediately following the incident, he told Hickman and Roth to meet him at a place called "Rolf" at Paso Robles, about 150 miles north. Apparently, he planned on putting some distance between himself and the sluggish station wagon.

He did just that. And quickly.

Dean passed Bakersfield on Highway 466, which is now called Highway 46, and he and Wütherich stopped at a gas station called Blackwell's Corners. Dean ate an apple and had a coke, unaware that he only had a couple of hours to live. While he was near Highway 466 and Highway 33, he also encountered a couple of racing friends, Lance Reventlow and Bruce Kessler, who told him that they had both received tickets for speeding that day as well. That makes three! It almost seems as if something had been trying to warn Dean about the importance of slowing down...warning him about what was to come if he didn't. An angel perhaps?

Maybe, because after the station wagon finally arrived at the predetermined meeting place, Hickman again warned Dean about the necessity of slowing down. Only this time it was apparent that Hickman had Dean's safety on his mind, something he clearly told the actor, adding that he could hardly see the Spyder because of its colour and low height. The vehicle actually seemed to blend in with the silvery grey highway around it.

Yet again, James failed to heed Bill's warning, and when he returned to the Porsche, he rapidly accelerated on the highway in typical fashion. Not wearing his seatbelt, it was about 5:30 when he came to the crossing of Highway 466 and 41 at the east of the town Cholame. The area was known as being dangerous, because it harboured a notorious "black spot," yet Dean was driving at about 100 m/ph, the sunset bright in his eyes and nearly blinding.

John R. White, was driving on the highway when Dean quickly passed him up, the silver Spyder seeming like a silver bullet zipping across the ribbon of concrete. He also saw the black and white Ford Sedan up ahead that was coming from the opposite direction. Apparently the driver of the 1950 Ford Tudor, Donald Turnupseed, wanted to make a left turn and had to cut across Dean's path.

James also saw the other car. He told Wütherich, "That guy has to stop!"

Unfortunately, though Turnupseed did see the Spyder, there was no time to stop.

He tried to do so. *Desperately*! But even after he had floored the brakes of the Ford, the car continued to roll 30 feet onto the highway. The resulting collision was swift and violent. Though the left front fender of the Ford barely touched the Porsche, it was enough to send the 1,500 pound Spyder 49 feet into the air. Rolf, also not wearing a seatbelt, was brutally ejected from the convertible, his jaw-bone broken and his left thigh-bone shattered.

But James got it much worse.

The Spyder had crushed like a tin-can, burying him in sharp, twisted metal, and he sustained massive head injuries. About an hour later, he died en route to the emergency room, and was later pronounced dead at the Paso Robles Hospital.

Amazingly, Turnupseed survived the accident, yet, he was forever marred by the experience. He spent the rest of his life in Tulare and refused to comment about what happened that horrible night. It would be interesting to know if the Dean "curse" continued to touch his life following the accident...like it had so many others, Rolf Wütherich included.

Though Wütherich had survived the accident, he never really fully recuperated physically from the injuries, and after he returned to Germany, he died in 1981, ironically, from a car accident.

Needless to say, like so many others, he probably wished that he had never seen or had anything to do with that car. And even worse, the evil force of the car didn't stop with Dean's death. The "Little Bastard" continued to kill and maim.

The "bad luck" that seemed to virtually exude from the hunk of twisted metal was still alive and well in March, 1959, when a fire broke out in the Fresno garage where it had been stored. But that was just the beginning of the accidents and disasters that would be associated with the vehicle.

A few weeks later, there would be another incident.

In 1959, the Dean mania was still intense, the accident still fresh on everyone's mind. Thus, the California State Highway Patrol had the mangled vehicle transported to local high schools to teach teenagers the importance of safe driving. Since Dean was supposedly driving at between 85-100 m/ph during the accident, it seemed that the crushed Porsche would serve as a good example of the dangers of high speed driving.

But they would eventually come to regret that decision. When the Porsche was near Salinas, the vehicle transporting it was involved in a serious accident. The impact was so great that truck driver, George Barhuis, was thrown from the cab. In response, the Porsche rolled off the truck bed, landed on top of him and literally crushed him to death, claiming another victim.

Despite the latest tragedy, the exhibit was, nevertheless, popular. People came in droves to see the James Dean car, and the owner, George Barris (a name that's amazingly similar to that of the car's second victim) decided that the tour would extend to the other states as well.

Of course, there would be another accident.

On September 30, the anniversary of Dean's death, a fifteen-year-old boy became the car's next victim. He was standing about twelve to fifteen feet away from the exhibit, probably staring at it in shock and awe, when three bolts suddenly snapped as if broken by spectral hands. The boy screamed as the car ploughed forward and ran over him. Both of the boy's legs were horribly crushed, but he survived.

The next victim would not be so lucky.

A few weeks later the death car was again being transported when it caused yet another mishap. This time, it literally snapped in two, slid from the flatbed of the truck, and met the grey pavement. The wreckage caused another fatal accident before it could be cleared from the roadway.

In 1960, the owner, had finally had enough, and he decided to have the Porsche shipped back home to California for a permanent retirement. The car was loaded into a boxcar in Florida, the door carefully sealed. When the train arrived in Los Angeles, the seal on the boxcar door was still intact – *yet the Porsche was missing!*

Despite the efforts of detectives, the car has never been located. Maybe it returned to the hell from whence it came. Or, could it be in some secret place today – still killing and wounding, and spreading bad luck to all those who encounter it?

Some believe, however, that whatever curse was placed on Dean touched not only his car, but also those he was closest to.

All three lead actors from *Rebel Without A Cause* had tragic deaths at a young age. Sal Mineo, one of Dean's best friends, was only 37 in 1975 when he was stabbed to death in West Hollywood Alley. Another friend and co-star of Dean's in the blockbuster movie, Natalie Wood, was only 43 years old when she drowned in a tragic boating accident. Nick Adams, who also played a part in the movie, though it was a bit part, later went on to become "Johnny Reb" in a popular weekly television series; however, his career came to a quick end when he died at only 36 from an overdose.

Indeed, if Dean and the Porsche were cursed, how did this come about? Who in the world would want to curse the actor anyway? It seemed that everyone loved and adored him, young and old alike.

A lot of people would swear that there wasn't a curse at all, but that there was a malevolent spirit in that Porsche – a spirit that had been there all along. Or the car itself might have been evil, similar to the Chrysler Fury in Stephen King's *Christine*. Others would swear that Dean's death resulted from his involvement in the occult and a flirtation with Satanism, since he was also involved with a witch coven in Los Angeles.

Dean supposedly became interested in the occult when he dated Maila Nurmi, an actress who starred in *Vampira*. Because Dean was afraid that the affair could negatively affect his career, he publicly denied any romantic involvement with Nurmi. In fact, he told gossip columnist Hedda Hoppe that he'd never dated Nurmi.

Rumour has it that Nurmi didn't take this public spurning well, and as a result, she supposedly cast a black magic spell on Dean.

Or was one of the other witches he met responsible?

Whatever killed James Dean, his life and his death is something that the world will never forget. Andy Warhol said it best in *Interview Magazine*: "He's not our hero because he was perfect, but because he perfectly represented the damaged, but beautiful soul of his time."

Whatever the source of the appeal, the Dean mania continues, and thousands of fans who virtually worship the man, meet regularly at his burial site at the Fairmount Cemetery in Indiana, and there are rumours that the supernatural phenomena concerning James Dean continues.

Many of his fans would swear that James Dean has returned from the grave. And there have been reports of a spectral Porsche cruising the highway in the area where Dean was killed. And exactly where is that Porsche Spyder or for that matter James Dean's body? Someone supposedly stole the corpse from the grave, and more recently, his headstone was taken as well, though it was quickly returned. Little wonder that Dean might be disturbed enough to walk the earth again.

50. Castle of Fate?

Would anyone dream of a fairytale castle as being jinxed? Probably not, but the beautiful castle of Miramar near Trieste seems to have brought bad luck to those who lived in it. Miramar Castle was built in the mid-19th century by the Archduke Maximilian, a younger brother of the Emperor Franz Josef of Austria-Hungary. Maximilian had once been blown ashore near Trieste while sailing in a small boat, and some fishermen gave him shelter. Inspired by the beauty of the place, he decided that day to make his home there. Later he built a white palace with delicate towers, terraces of granite, and flights of marble steps leading down to a landing stage guarded by sphinxes. The garden was planted with firs and flowering trees, and visitors described it as one of the most beautiful places on earth. The first owner started the catalogue of misfortunes connected with Miramar. It was there that Maximilian accepted the fatal offer of the imperial crown of Mexico, which resulted in his death in front of a Mexican firing squad three years later. His wife Carlotta, who was only 26, went insane.

The Empress Elisabeth, wife of Franz Josef, was the next resident of Miramar, living there with her son Rudolf. Rudolf came to a tragic end in 1889 by committing suicide with his beloved, and the Empress was assassinated in 1898 by an Italian anarchist who believed in Italian liberation from Austria. The next to live at Miramar was Archduke Franz Ferdinand, Rudolf's cousin and heir to the imperial throne. He and his wife were assassinated in Sarajevo, starting the jinx of the car as well. At the end of World War I, when Trieste passed from Austrian to Italian hands, the Duke of Aosta, a cousin of the King of Italy, moved into Miramar. He died in a prison camp in Kenya during World War II. After that, two British Major Generals became residents of the castle of Miramar. Both died of heart attacks.

51. Don't Touch Me or My Objects

The destructive power of a curse is real and undisputed. People who believe they are under a curse to die will often obediently proceed to die. Those most likely to react in this way are primitive peoples whose lives are rigorously ordered by ritual and taboo. Such were the Maoris of New Zealand, and such still are many Amazon Indians of South America. In earlier times a Maori chief was a sacred figure, and it was taboo to touch him or objects that had belonged to him. It was accepted that any transgression would be punished by the angered ancestral spirits of the tribe. Sir James Frazer in *The Golden Bough* tells of a Maori warrior who unwittingly ate the unfinished dinner of his chief. When he learned what he had done, he was immediately seized by violent stomach cramps and convulsion. He died of the seizures at sundown the same day. Knowing he was fated to die, his body and mind combined to bring his death about.

52. The Cursed Ship - *Great Republic*

There are several ships which have acquired reputations for being unlucky. Numerous accidents happen to these ships and bad fortune seems to follow them. Though there is no reason for certain ships to be cursed or jinxed, the belief that some are is widespread.

Great Republic seemed to be dogged by bad luck. This great American sailing ship was launched on October 4, 1853. Many old sailors who watched the ceremony were filled with foreboding. Instead of wine, the ship was launched with a bottle of water because of the influence of the local temperance league.

Within weeks of launching, the *Great Republic* was reduced almost to a wreck by a devastating fire. She was rebuilt and sent to sea. Soon a succession of accidents gave the ship the reputation of being unlucky. On one particularly ominous occasion, a sailor died of an unknown disease. The burial service was read by the captain and the man's body tipped overboard. Immediately a freak wave washed the corpse back on board.

The ship eventually foundered for no apparent cause after 19 years of bad luck and fatal accidents. Such a succession of misfortunes could be explained away as mere coincidence. However, many people, particularly those who spend their lives at sea, firmly believe that certain ships are jinxed and are followed by bad luck.

53. "Cannibal" Victim Had His Revenge

Only four men escaped when the British square-rigged yacht *Pierrot* capsized in the Atlantic Ocean in July 1884. Huddled in a battered dinghy, they drifted for 25 days. Near death from starvation and exposure, Captain Edwin Rutt then made a last desperate suggestion.

Lots should be drawn to determine which of the four would be eaten.

Two of the sailors agreed with Rutt, but 18-year-old Dick Tomlin, the youngest crewman, protested that he would rather die than eat human flesh.

Tomlin's resistance sealed his fate. At the first opportunity Rutt crept towards the sleeping boy and drove a knife into his neck.

The mate Josh Dudley and seaman Will Hoon had no reservations about cannibalism. When they were rescued by the yacht *Gellert* four days later, it was the slain boy's flesh that had sustained them.

The horror-stricken master of the *Gellert* rejected the idea of burial at sea. Hidden away underneath a tarpaulin, the body of the victim accompanied the three survivors to the Cornish port of Falmouth.

All three were tried and condemned to death for murder on the high seas. But the Home Secretary decided that there had been horror enough and commuted the sentence to six months' imprisonment.

No one could have known that the horrors were only beginning.

When the three men were freed from jail, they found little future. To keep body and soul together, Josh Dudley found work as a drayman. Two weeks later his team of horses saw something that frightened them in the middle of a foggy London street. Bolting, they tossed Dudley to the cobblestones where his head shattered.

Witnesses said the thing in the fog had been a figure swathed from head to foot in bloodstained bandages. After Dudley's death, the figure mysteriously vanished.

With fear beginning to take root, Captain Rutt went to the Soho slums and sought out Will Hoon. He found the old seaman far gone in drink, a sodden derelict in desperately bad health.

Rutt told Hoon that some vengeance-crazed relative was masquerading as Dick Tomlin's ghost, and he urged Hoon to help him ferret out the plotter. But Hoon wanted only more gin, and in a last delirium, he was taken to the charity ward of a hospital where he died in a screaming fit.

Witnesses said later that another patient "dressed all in bandages" had been holding Hoon down, apparently trying to soothe him. Then the patient vanished.

Now in a state of abject terror, Rutt went to the police. They scoffed at his tales of a "figure in bandages". But in view of the captain's mental condition, they offered him one night of lodging in a cell.

Rutt went gratefully to the cell, checking twice to be sure he was locked in. It was a cell block for the disturbed of London, and screams in the night were not uncommon.

But when at 3 a.m. the police heard the captain, some distinctive quality in his cries brought warders running. They unlocked the door and went to his bunk, where Rutt lay with his knees scissored upward and his dead eyes like marbles.

Clenched in his fingers the shocked policemen saw shreds of cotton. And bloodstained gauze.

54. The Curse of Hitler's Yacht

A more direct curse seems to have followed the subsequent owners of Adolf Hitler's yacht, the *Ostwind.* Constructed on the Fuhrer's orders and designed to conquer all comers in international yacht races, the sleek, 26 m craft was launched just 3 days after the German Army invaded Poland. Opportunities for yacht racing stopped with the end of World War II, so rather than let the vessel sit idle, Hitler appropriated the *Ostwind* as his private pleasure boat.

In 1950, several years after the war's end, the US Navy sold the captured vessel to Commander John Lyman, a Navy officer and an avid yachtsman. He entered the *Ostwind* in races up and down the East Coast. But in Miami, a heavy piece of sailing gear mysteriously fell from the rigging and smashed his face. Seriously injured, Lyman sold the *Ostwind* to entrepreneurs who converted the craft into a sleazy imitation of its former majestic appearance.

A Daytona Beach attorney, horrified at the *Ostwind's* fate, bought the yacht with the intention of restoring it's fading glory. The vessel suddenly sank, and the attorney died less than a year later.

In 1971, Horace Glass, a Jacksonville advertising executive, raised the yacht and spent 10 years and over $110,000 in an effort to convert the *Ostwind* into a floating museum. But the curse caught up with him in 1982, when a storm undid all of Glass's costly restoration and left him financially drained.

In 1990, a Miami Beach politician took the rotting hulk out to sea and sank it, sending the curse to the bottom of the ocean along with the *Ostwind.*

55. The Curse of the Presidents

Is it a curse that decrees that every president of the United States elected in a year divisible by 20 will die in office? History shows that this has been the case since 1840. Three died naturally – William Henry Harrison, who was elected in 1840, Warren G. Harding (1920), and Franklin D. Roosevelt (1940). Assassins killed Abraham Lincoln (1860),

James A. Garfield (1880), William Mckinley (1900), and John F. Kennedy (1960). The pattern in itself is odd enough, but the fact that both assassinations and natural deaths fit into this pattern is odder still. When Roosevelt, first elected in 1932 and re-elected in 1936 and 1940, survived to the end of his third term, it might have been thought that the jinx had been lifted. But it re-asserted itself during his fourth term. Re-elected in November 1944, he was dead the following spring.

No one can put a name to an apparent blight that strikes American presidents in given years.

56. Noose For A Strangler

George Gaffney was a petty thief. He operated from London's seedy Soho red-light district in the early years of this century. His crimes were all minor, except for one – and that was the most serious of all. On the first day of March 1910, Gaffney saw on a street-seller's cart a strange three-foot length of woven silk rope which he recognised as a "thuggee cord", used by the Hindu assassins' sect in the Middle East to dispatch their victims.

Gaffney bought it. Two weeks later, he used it...............

The cheap thief had been having problems with a girl named Bessie Graves, who expected him to marry her because she was pregnant. But Gaffney had wooed her under the alias of Arthur Eames. Now he had found a much more promising opportunity – an elderly rich widow, named Stella Fortney.

Called by a hysterical landlady, Scotland Yard detectives found Bessie Graves with the strangler's cord drawn so tightly around her throat it was embedded in the flesh. Their only clue was that the probable strangler was a man who called himself Arthur Eames.

It was little for the Yard to go on, and three weeks later Gaffney was still at large pursuing his romance with the widow.

It occurred to him one night that he would make a more impressive appearance if he called on the lady in a hansom cab. A second later he was screaming. In the half-light of the closed vehicle, George found Bessie Graves sharing the seat with him. The dead girl's eyes stared glassily into his, and the swollen tongue lolled from her mouth.

For more than a week Gaffney drank steadily, then he went to see Stella. She was far from friendly that evening, but melted when Gaffney gave her a stolen diamond ring. They shared a bottle of champagne, after which she sent him to the cellar for another. Bearing a kerosene lamp, Gaffney was halfway down the steps when Bessie Graves climbed out of the darkness to meet him.

She had succeeded in loosening the strangler's cord, which swung from her throat like a necklace. But the staring eyes were worse. Screaming Gaffney threw the lamp at her and crashed headlong to the bottom of the stairs.

Gaffney spent three weeks in hospital. And when he left he decided that he had only one chance of throwing off the ghost who would not leave him alone. If he put England behind him forever, perhaps Bessie Graves would remain there, too. He booked a passage on the liner *Montrose,* for Quebec.

With renewed hope he checked into a small hotel on the eve of the voyage. In the semi-gloom of the room, he saw Bessie again.

This time she had freed herself from the silken noose and was holding it out to him. Feebly, he took it from her clawlike fingers. When he lifted his eyes again, Bessie had vanished. But the message was obvious. Gaffney sat down and began to scrawl his confession.

He told in detail of Bessie's murder and of her successive visits from the tomb. And now, he said, there was no possible escape.

Called by hotel staff, men from the Yard broke into Gaffney's room. They found the thief hanging from a beam. They read his confession and agreed at once that the case of the Soho strangler was closed.

Yet there was one element of the case that puzzled them. For the first time, a vital piece of evidence had vanished from the Yard's thief-proof vaults. It was the thuggee cord – the same cord that Gaffney used to hang himself in the closet!

57. By Fire and Water

Battle Abbey in Sussex was the scene of a grim curse laid on the descendants of Sir Anthony Browne, 'Esquire to the Body of Henry VIII, Master of the Horse and Justice in Eyre', in 1538.

According to tradition, Sir Anthony was cursed at the feast held to celebrate his ownership of the abbey by a monk who was angry at the seizure of Church lands during the Reformation.

The curse was specific: the family would die 'by fire or water'. It seems, however, that the curse went awry: Sir Anthony's other property, Cowdray Park – which he had inherited from his half-cousin, the Earl of Southhampton – was burned down; but this was much later, in 1793, after the property had passed into the hands of another family.

Anthony Hippisley Coxe, compiler of *Haunted Britain* (1974), records that the curse came unstuck yet again, in 1907, when the Duchess of Cleveland – who had rented Battle Abbey briefly – drowned in its grounds on her way to church, but her daughter, who was with her, survived.

58. Skull of Horror

Lieutenant Commander "Buster" Crabbe dived with Royal Navy men in 1950 in Tobermory Bay, Isle of Mull, in search of the *Duque de Florencia*, a payship of the Spanish Armada, which had been sunk in 1588 with a reputed 30 million pounds of gold on board. One of the trophies with which he surfaced was a skull that medical experts said had belonged to a North American woman. Crabbe disappeared, some maintain mysteriously, while on an underwater mission near Russian warships in Portsmouth harbour in 1956. The following year a coroner decided that the headless body of a frogman washed up at Chichester, Sussex, was that of Crabbe.

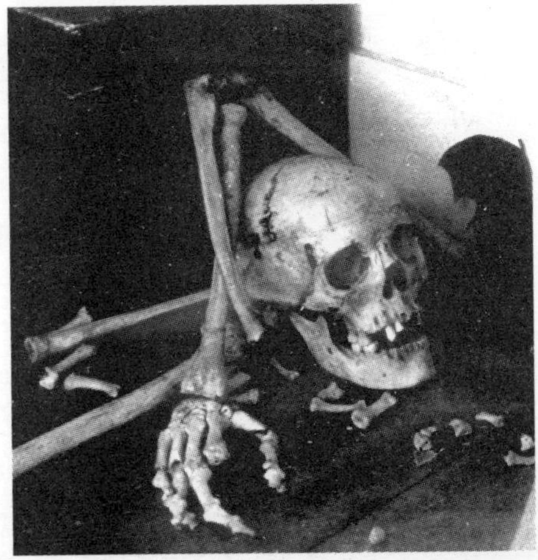

The skull that had been found on the wreck was kept in the Western Isles Hotel, Tobermory, Scotland, where one day the barman accidentally caused it to fall and break. The same day he crashed his motor scooter and cracked *his* skull. He never returned to the island. The hotel owner, Donald Maclean, stored the skull away in a cupboard. In 1970 Richard Forrester, the new English owner of the hotel, drilled a hole in the skull so that he could hang it up in his cocktail bar:

'I was using an ordinary electrical drill. The first odd thing that happened was that the metal bit of the drill, after piercing the bone, bent inside at an angle of 45 degrees. I found this surprising but thought nothing more about it. Two hours later I was struck by excruciating pain in the back of the head. I was completely incapacitated for two days. Since then I have been taking prescribed pills but the searing pain continues and never leaves.'

And the only other person to handle the skull since the drilling had also experienced searing headaches.

59. The Ship That Sailed Itself

Some ships just seem cursed with bad luck. The *Amazon* was christened in 1861 at Spencer Island, Nova Scotia, and just 48 hours after taking command of the ship, its captain suddenly died. On its maiden voyage, the *Amazon* struck a fishing weir (a fence), leaving a gash in its hull. While being repaired, the ship suffered a fire which broke out on board. Not long after, during its third Atlantic crossing, the *Amazon* collided with another ship. Finally, in 1867, the ill-fated ship was wrecked off the coast of Newfoundland and abandoned for salvagers. But the ship had one last date with destiny. It was raised and restored by an American company who sailed it south for sale. It was purchased in 1872 by Captain Benjamin S. Briggs who raised its sails and headed out to sea towards the Mediterranean with his family – only now the ship was renamed the *Mary Celeste!*

On December 3, 1872, the crew of the *Dei Gratia*, sailing from New York to Gibraltar, found the *Mary Celeste* floating unmanned about 600 miles west of Portugal. The ship was in perfect condition. The sails were set, its cargo of 1,700 barrels of commercial alcohol were untouched (except for one barrel, which had been opened), a breakfast meal looked as though it been abandoned in the middle of being eaten, and all of the crew's belongings remained onboard. Yet its captain, Benjamin S. Briggs, his wife, his daughter, and the ship's crew of seven were gone. Some versions of the story say that the ship's lifeboat was missing, while others say it was still in place on deck. All that seemed to be missing was the ship's chronometer, the sextant, and the cargo documents. There was no sign of a struggle, violence, storm, or any other kind of disturbance. The last entry in the ship's log was made on November 24, and made no indication of any trouble. If this ship had been abandoned soon after this entry, the *Mary Celeste* would have been adrift for a week and a half. But this was impossible, according to the crew of the *Dei Gratia,* considering the ship's position and the way its sails had been set. Someone – or something – must have worked the ship for at least several days after the final log entry. The fate of the crew of the *Mary Celeste* remains a mystery.

60. The Curse of Tutankhamun

Of the original team of archaeologists who were present when the ancient tomb of the boy king Tutankhamun was opened, only one lived to a ripe old age. Was this a bizarre coincidence? Or was it the manifestation of a curse that had passed down through the centuries – a curse too sinister, too mysterious and too lethal for the modern world to comprehend? And a curse that is still exacting its deadly toll today....

The final wall of the sealed burial chamber of the boy pharaoh was breached for the first time in 3,000 years on February 17, 1923. Archaeologist Howard Carter whispered breathlessly that he could see 'things, wonderful things' as he gazed in awe at the treasures of Tutankhamun. As Carter, together with fanatical Egyptologist Lord Carnarvon, looked at the treasures of gold, gems, precious stones and other priceless relics, they ignored the dire warning written all those centuries ago to ward off grave robbers. In the ancient hieroglyphics above their heads, it read:

'Death will come to those who disturb the sleep of the pharaohs.'

The final blow of the excavators' pick had set free the Curse of the Pharaoh. Lord Carnarvon had never taken lightly the threats of ancient Egypt's high priests. In England before his expedition had set out, he had consulted a famous mystic of the day, Count Hamon, who warned him:

'Lord Carnarvon not to enter tomb. Disobey at peril. If ignored will suffer sickness. Not recover. Death will claim him in Egypt.'

Two separate visits to mediums in England had also prophesied his impending doom. But for Carter and Lord Carnarvon, who had financed the dig culminating in history's greatest archaeological find, all thoughts of curses and hocus-pocus were forgotten as they revelled in the joy of the victorious end to the dig. The site of Luxor had escaped the attentions of grave robbers down through the centuries, and the treasure-packed tomb was a find beyond compare.

The accolades of the world's academics rained down on him and his team. The praise of museums and seats of learning as far apart as Cairo and California was heaped on them. Carnarvon revelled in the glittering prize of fame – little knowing that he had but two months to enjoy the fruits of his success. On April 5, 1923, just 47 days after breaching the chamber into Tutankhamun's resting place, Carnarvon, aged 57, died in agony – the victim, apparently, of an infected mosquito bite. At the moment of his death in the Continental Hotel, Cairo, the lights in the city went out in unison, and stayed off for some minutes. And if further proof were needed that it was indeed a strange force that was at work, thousands of miles away in England, at Lord Carnarvon's country house, his dog began baying and howling – a blood-curdling, unnatural lament which shocked the domestic staff deep in the middle of the night. It continued until one last whine, when the tormented creature turned over and died.

The newspapers of the day were quick to speculate that such eerie happenings were caused by the curse, an untapped source of evil which Carnarvon and Carter had unleashed. Their sensational conclusion was reinforced when, two days after Carnarvon's death, the mummified body of the pharaoh was examined and a blemish was found on his left cheek exactly in the position of the mosquito bite on Carnarvon's face. Perhaps this could have been passed off as coincidence had it not been for the bizarre chain of deaths that were to follow.

Shortly after Carnarvon's demise, another archaeologist, Arthur Mace, a leading member of the expedition, went into a coma at the Hotel Continental after complaining of tiredness. He died soon afterwards, leaving the expedition medic and local doctors baffled. The deaths continued. A close friend of Carnarvon, George Gould, made the voyage to Egypt when he learned of his fate. Before leaving the port to travel to Cairo he looked in at the tomb. The following day he collapsed with a high fever; twelve hours later he was dead.

Radiologist Archibald Reid, a man who used the latest X-ray techniques to determine the age and possible cause of death of Tutankhamun, was sent back to England after complaining of exhaustion. He died soon after landing.

Carnarvon's personal secretary, Richard Bethell, was found dead in bed from heart failure four months after the discovery of the tomb. The casualties continued to mount. Joel Wool, a leading British industrialist of the time, visited the site and was dead a few months later from a fever which doctors could not comprehend.

Six years after the discovery, twelve of those present when the tomb was opened were dead. Within a further seven years only two of the original team of excavators were still alive. Lord Carnarvon's half-brother apparently took his own life while temporarily insane, and a further 21 people connected in some way with the dig, were also dead. Of the original pioneers of the excavation, only Howard Carter lived to a ripe old age, dying in 1939 from natural causes. Others have not been so fortunate.

While countless Egyptologists and academics have tried to debunk the legend of the curse as pure myth, others have continued to fall victim to it's influence.

Mohammed Ibrahim, Egypt's director of antiquities, in 1966 argued with the government against letting the treasures from the tomb leave Egypt for an exhibition in Paris. He pleaded with the authorities to allow the relics to stay in Cairo because he had suffered terrible nightmares of what would happen to him if they left the country. Ibrahim left a final meeting with the government officials, stepped out into what looked like a clear road on a bright sunny day, was hit by a car and died instantly.

Perhaps even more bizarre was the case of Richard Adamson who by 1969 was the sole surviving member of the 1923 expedition. Adamson had lost his wife within 24 hours of speaking out against the curse. His son broke his back in an aircraft crash when he spoke out again. Still sceptical, Adamson, who had worked as a security guard for Lord Carnarvon, defied the curse and gave an interview on British television, in which he still said that he did not believe in the curse. Later that evening, as he left the television studios, he was thrown from his taxi when it crashed, a swerving lorry missed his head by inches, and he was put in hospital with fractures and bruises. It was only then that the stoic Mr. Adamson, then aged 70, was forced to admit: 'Until now I refused to believe that my family's misfortunes had anything to do with the curse. But now I am not so sure.'

Perhaps the most amazing manifestation of the curse came in 1972, when the treasures of the tomb were transported to London for a prestigious exhibition at the British Museum. Victim number one was Dr. Gamal Mehrez, Ibrahim's successor in Cairo as director of antiquities. He scoffed at the legend, saying that his whole life had been spent in Egyptology and that all the deaths and misfortune through the decades had been the result of 'pure coincidence'. He died the night after supervising the packaging of the relics for transport to England by a Royal Air Force plane.

The crew members of that aircraft suffered death, injury, misfortune and disaster in the years that followed their cursed flight. Flight Lieutenant Rick Laurie died in 1976 from a heart attack. His wife declared:

'It's the curse of Tutankhamun – the curse has killed him.'

Ken Parkinson, a flight engineer, suffered a heart attack each year at the same time as the flight aboard the Britannia aircraft which brought the treasures to England until a final fatal one in 1978. Before their mission to Egypt neither of the servicemen had suffered any heart trouble, and had been pronounced fit by military doctors. During the flight, Chief Technical Officer Ian Lansdown kicked the crate that contained the death mask of the boy king, 'I've just kicked the most expensive thing in the world,' he quipped. Later on disembarking from the aircraft on another mission, a ladder mysteriously broke beneath him and the leg he had kicked the crate with was badly broken. It was in plaster for nearly six months.

Flight Lieutenant Jim Webb, who was aboard the aircraft, lost everything he owned after a fire devastated his home. A steward, Brian Rounsfall, confessed to playing cards on the sarcophagus of Tutankhamun on the flight home and suffered two heart attacks. And a woman officer on board the plane was forced to leave the RAF after having a serious operation.

The mystery remains. Were all those poor souls down the years merely the victims of some gigantic set of coincidences? Or did the priestly guardians of the tomb's dark secrets really exert supernatural forces which heaped so much misery and suffering on those who invaded their sacred chambers – and exact a terrible punishment on the despoilers of the magnificent graves of their noble dead?

The most intriguing theory to explain the legend of the curse was advanced by atomic scientist Louis Bulgarini in 1949. He wrote:

'It is definitely possible that the ancient Egyptians use atomic radiation to protect their holy places. The floors of the tombs could have been covered with uranium. Or the graves could have been finished with radioactive rock. Rock containing both gold and uranium was mined in Egypt. Such radiation could kill a man today.'

61. Dudleytown

Dudleytown is an abandoned 18th century village in the woods of Cornwall, Connecticut. Though controversial with historians and genealogists, Dudleytown is one of the most intriguing haunted sites in America.

The first settler in Dudleytown was Thomas Griffis, who acquired the first plot of land in about 1738. Others, including the men of the Dudley family, bought land and settled in the area around Griffis during the mid-1740s. The people in the area helped to support themselves by cutting lumber to fuel iron production in a nearby town. Life for these early residents was difficult. The soil in the area is rocky and acidic. Being in the shadow of three mountains Dudleytown receives little sun.

The intriguing part comes from the curse that many believe the Dudley family brought with them when they came from England. This is also where various sources begin to disagree. Some say that the Dudleys came from a long line of damned people, including a primary carrier of the Bubonic Plague and a Lord who lost his head along with Lady Jane Grey. Others believe that the Dudleys tangled with powerful royals who arranged to have a curse put on them. (This is also the reason given as to why they left England.) People also think that the land itself was spiritually unsettled long before the town was founded.

Though it is assumed that Abiel, Barzallai, Gideon, and Abijah Dudley were all brothers, there is no proof. At any rate, Abiel is the first brother to appear in the records, having been listed in tax records from 1744. Abiel was also one of the first victims of the curse, losing his mind as well as his money. He lived hand to mouth for the rest of his life, doing odd jobs for the townspeople in order to earn his keep.

Insanity, murder and suicide were rapidly becoming a staple of life in Dudleytown. The first recorded fatality happened in 1792, when Gershom Hollister fell while repairing a barn. Hollister is believed to have been murdered by William Tanner, who owned the barn. Tanner soon went insane due to the controversy.

Just after moving away from Dudleytown in 1763, most of the Nathaniel Carter family was wiped out by Indians. In 1804, Sara Faye Swift was struck by lightning and killed.

Her husband, General Herman Swift (a veteran of the Revolutionary War) went crazy afterwards. Dudleytown's most famous resident Mary Cheney (wife of Horace Greeley) hung herself in 1872.

Many strange tales were told about Dudleytown during the 19th century.

People reported seeing strange beasts and apparitions. Corpse mutilations were reported, along with still more suspicious and unusual deaths. Soon people began to give up on Dudleytown, and it was mostly deserted by 1900.

However, people still tried to live in Dudleytown. During the 1920s Dr. William C. Clark set up a summer home in the abandoned town. One evening he came back from a business trip to find his wife laughing hysterically. She told her husband about the apparitions and demons that had visited while he was absent. She killed herself when they returned to New York. Ironically, Dr. Williams remarried and continued to spend his summers in Dudleytown. In fact, he formed the Dark Entry Forest Association, which helps to protect Dudleytown's remains.

Many visitors today often report lots of disembodied voices whispering and laughing. A woman on a white horse has been spotted among other apparitions. People also hear wagon wheels and other sounds of the past. The one thing that people do not hear in Dudleytown are birds and other life sounds. Living animals seem to flee the area. Some believe that this area is a vortex, or simply an area of negative energy that attracts unpleasant spirits and people.

Dudleytown can be difficult for visitors. The site is considered dangerous because many people report getting minor injuries, being pushed and shoved by unseen hands, or simply overcome by feelings of despair.

62. The *Great Eastern*

One of the most notorious jinx ship of the 19th century – the British vessel *Great Eastern* was built by the famous British engineer Isambard Kingdom Brunel starting in 1854, and was one of his few failures. In its day the passenger liner was the largest – and the unluckiest – ship in the world. The vessel was planned to be the wonder of the seas, a floating palace carrying 4000 passengers in luxury around the world. The six masts and five funnels were more than any other ship had ever carried. Marine jargon did not have enough names for so many masts, so they were referred to as Monday, Tuesday, Wednesday, Thursday, Friday, and Saturday. The colossal hull, 692 feet long, surpassed the dimensions of Noah's Ark. In fact, the *Great Eastern* had two hulls, one inside the other, three feet apart and heavily braced. Inside the hull, there was an ingenious arrangement of longitudinal and transverse bulkheads, forming

16 watertight compartments. This was designed to make it virtually unsinkable – and it is true that while nearly every other calamity befell the ship, it never sank.

Hammering in the three million rivets, each one an inch thick and all driven in by hand, took 200 rivet gangs 1000 work days. Fatal accidents during construction were fewer than average – four workers and a spectator. But one riveter and his apprentice disappeared, and there was a rumour that they had been sealed up in a hull compartment and that their screams for help had been drowned in the din of the hammers.

The original backers ran out of money when the price of iron plate increased, and work stopped till Brunel had succeeded in raising more money. Launching the heaviest hull in history into the Thames river had to be performed sideways. It took an agonising three months to get the vessel to move the 330 feet down to the water. Chains snapped, barges sank, innumerable hydraulic rams burst under the strain. Day after day Brunel worked to inch his giant structure a few feet closer to the water. The *Times* correspondent in London wrote: "There she lies on the very brink of the noble river which is to carry her to the ocean, but she will not wet her lips." When the launch was finally made on the last day of January 1858, it had cost £ 1000 a foot.

Total expenses had already reached over £ 1 million. The cost of completing the ship broke the next company, but once more Brunel managed to raise the money to carry on. The new board of directors set aside the original plan to take the *Great Eastern* on long voyages to India and Australia – for which the liner was uniquely suitable. Instead, they went after the quick profits of a North Atlantic run. Only the first class cabins were completed for the maiden voyage, the second and third class accommodation left for what turned out to be another nine years. The day before the great ship was to sail, Brunel came down for an inspection. The famous engineer was prematurely aged at 53. Just after posing with colleagues for a photograph, he staggered and collapsed with a stroke. Brunel died a week later as news came through that one of the *Great Eastern*'s funnels had exploded as the liner steamed down the Channel, because a steam valve had been left closed. Five men were scalded to death and another fell to his death in one of the great paddle wheels. The grand salon with its mirrored walls and sumptuous decoration was wrecked.

Repairs took longer than expected and the planned voyage to the United States was cancelled. In order to get some return on their investment, the directors moved the by-then notorious ship to Holyhead, Wales and opened it to sightseers. Not long after, a howling gale tore it from its moorings and drove it out to sea. For 18 hours the vessel rode the storm while many nearby ships sank, proving how well it was designed. But the recently repaired salon was ruined again. Three months later the captain, the coxswain, and the nine-year-old son of the chief purser were drowned when a sudden squall upset their gig as they were going ashore.

Nothing casts a sharper blight over a ship's character than the death of the captain during or before a maiden voyage. When the news reached London the directors of the *Great Eastern*'s managing company resigned. The next board set a definite sailing date of June 9, 1860, but June 9 came and went. Most of the 300 ticketed passengers – all that the ship had beds for – tired of waiting and sailed on one of Sir Samuel Cunard's more reliable ships. When the *Great Eastern* finally left Southampton on June 16, only 35 paying passengers were aboard. The new captain, commanding a crew of 418, had never crossed the Atlantic Ocean before.

During the 12-day crossing the cheap coal that was being used as an economy measure damaged the funnel casings and made the main dining room so hot that passengers refused to sit there. Otherwise the voyage was uneventful, and the huge liner arrived to a sensational welcome in New York. However, sightseers, incensed at the high $ 1 admission fee charged for visiting on board, tried to get their money's worth by pocketing souvenirs. Later, an announced two-day excursion turned into a nightmare. Two thousand people were faced with the problem of sleeping on only 300 beds. A pipe burst in the storage room and flooded the food supplies, leaving nothing available to eat except dessicated chicken, salted meat, and stone-hard biscuits. For this passengers were charged outrageous prices. Most of the passengers had to spend the night on the deck, where they had the unpleasant experience of being covered by cinders raining down from the five funnels. In the morning there was no water to wash off the grit. The passengers thought they could at least look forward to a speedy landing, but by some error of navigation the *Great Eastern* had gone off course during the night and was 100 miles out to sea. There was no food left for breakfast or lunch. When land was at last reached, the hungry, grimy, weary passengers fought to disembark.

A second excursion was announced, but not surprisingly, only a handful of tickets were bought. New York was disenchanted with the great ship. Almost unnoticed it left for England with 90 passengers on board. But the return trip was not to be without incident either. In mid-Atlantic a screw shaft gave out. At Milford Haven the vessel fouled the hawser of a small boat and drowned two of its passengers. Then the huge liner crashed into the frigate *Blenheim*.

The next captain, the third, never sailed, resigning rather than sail short-handed when the directors fired one-third of the crew. Under the fourth captain, the ship sailed with only 100 passengers, even though there were 300 emigrants willing to travel steerage. In fact, the *Great Eastern* never carried any emigrants across the Atlantic, although in this respect it could have beaten all competition and made great profits. The owners single-mindedly concentrated on first-class passengers during the nine years before second and third class accommodation was installed – and the ship never came near getting a full complement of such travellers. Profits were also hindered because the vessel was too cold to cross the Atlantic in the winter.

In September 1861, the *Great Eastern* was struck by a hurricane that would probably have sunk any other vessel. Both the side paddles were ripped off. All lifeboats were torn away.

The rudder broke and began crashing against the screw. Repairs cost £ 60,000. The following year in Long Island Sound the ship struck a tall needle of rock unmarked on the charts; it tore a rip 83 feet long and 9 feet wide in the other hull. This time repairs cost £ 70,000.

In 1864, the unlucky ship was put up for auction and bought for £ 25,000 to begin a new career as a cable layer. Misfortune still hounded it. When 1186 miles out from Ireland on the way to Newfoundland, an accident caused the cable to slip and the severed end sank three miles to the ocean bed. All efforts to recover it failed, so the ship returned to England. Another try in 1866 was successful, and on July 27 the first messages by undersea cable passed between Europe and North America.

As a vessel for laying cable, the *Great Eastern* at last justified its existence. In 1869 it sailed for India – the only time it visited the latitudes it had been designed for – and laid a cable between Bombay (Mumbai) and Aden.

In 1874 the launching of the first custom-built cable ships brought an end to the only profitable employment the *Great Eastern* ever enjoyed. A mere 15 years after being launched, the great ship was brought back to Milford Haven where it remained rusting and blocking the shipping lines for the next 12 years. By 1886 the barnacles on the hull were six inches thick. In that year the owners managed to sell the onetime liner for £ 20,000, and it was gingerly taken around the coast of Wales to Liverpool. There the *Great Eastern* damaged the tug *Wrestler*, the last boat it was to crash into. Then this former "Wonder of the Sea," this "Floating Palace," was painted with slogans advertising a Liverpool store. Later the vessel was taken to Dublin to advertise a brand of tea. Finally, a firm of metal dealers bought the down-at-heel ship. It had been sold for the last time.

Breaking up the *Great Eastern* proved almost as difficult as building it. In fact, the wrecker's iron ball, suspended on a giant chain, had to be invented for the purpose in 1889. Inside the double hull, demolition experts discovered two skeletons – the riveter and his boy apprentice, who had vanished when the ship was being built. Few people doubted that they had discovered the cause of the ship's jinx.

63. Annie Palmer and Rose Hall

Annie Palmer is said to be of mixed English and Irish descent. There are no pictures of her, but she is rumoured to have been rather short (under five feet) with dark hair. Some have said that she was pretty. Annie's parents were missionaries in Haiti, which is where she was raised. Annie spent a lot of her time with a native Haitian voodoo priestess who taught her the black arts.

Annie married John Palmer at 18 and moved to Jamaica with him. The house she became mistress of is one of the few surviving Great Houses. Apparently, Annie did not enjoy married life with John. Some accounts say that he beat her, and others say that he learned she had taken a slave as her lover. Regardless of the reason, Annie poisoned John Palmer. Annie later married two other men, both of whom died under mysterious circumstances. Annie claimed that they suffered from mortal illnesses, and quarantined the bodies. She later had them carried out and buried by slaves, who disappeared afterward. It is believed that she had the slaves killed so they couldn't tell anyone about the true cause of death. Interestingly, each husband lived and died in a different bedroom.

One of the most widely-held beliefs is the certainty that Annie enjoyed torturing her slaves. She had a small second-story balcony on the rear of the house, where she would stand and watch slaves being beaten or whipped, often to death. Naturally, the slaves were terrified of her and wished to be free from her. One story tells of a servant girl who tried to poison her. The attempt was unsuccessful. Annie was aware of her slaves' fear and often had a cat test the food before she ate. This seems to be what she did this time, and discovered the plot. Annie had the servant tried and executed, but requested that the girl's head be returned to her. She kept the head on a stick outside as a warning to the other slaves.

Annie is said to have enjoyed riding horseback at night. She often rode through the countryside and mercilessly whipped any slaves she found outside after dark. The native Jamaicans also claim that she used her voodoo powers to create monstrous apparitions, often in the form of menacing animals. The stories say that she would be seen in the area shortly before or after the apparitions. These apparitions often appeared when the slaves met for celebrations or to conspire against their mistress.

The most complete account of life at Rose Hall comes from the journal of a young bookkeeper who was sent to work at the plantation to learn the process before taking over one of his father's plantations. This young man was much admired by Annie, who desired to take him as her lover. Unfortunately for her, the bookkeeper fell in love with a servant who cleaned his house. When Annie learned why the bookkeeper discouraged her advances, she became very angry and put a curse on the servant girl. The servant girl became very afraid and told her uncle about the curse. Her uncle practiced the white magic side of voodoo, but was not powerful enough to lift the curse. The servant girl died soon after. Her uncle became very upset and held a meeting with a group of Annie's slaves. One night, the group (led by the uncle) raided the house. They found Annie in her bedroom and killed her. The young bookkeeper heard of the plot and went along, trying to stop the slaves before they killed Annie, but he was unsuccessful.

Afterward, the slaves burned some of Annie's belongings – particularly the pictures.

They were careful not to burn everything, and not to destroy the entire house because they were afraid that Annie's spirit would put a curse on all of them. Although damaged, Rose Hall remained standing.

After her death, Annie's slaves refused to bury her. Annie's neighbours eventually ordered their own servants to go and bury Annie on the plantation grounds. Annie's grave is still there, next to the house. When they marked the grave, they put crosses on all sides except one. Apparently, they weren't sure if Annie's spirit was inside or outside of the grave, and they didn't want to make her angry by locking her out of her resting place.

Rose Hall was left in ruins for many years. Local residents were afraid to move into the Great House, remembering Annie's declaration that it was her house, and no one else would ever have possession of it. After many years, a couple bought it and planned to restore it for themselves. While they were moving in, a servant woman fell from the observation balcony Annie used for witnessing whippings, and broke her neck. The fall was considered very mysterious due to the waist-high railing that encircles it. No one knows why the servant woman was on the balcony, but many believe that she was somehow lured there by Annie's spirit, and pushed over the railing.

Several years later, another couple bought the house. They carefully restored it and gave it to the Jamaican people as a historical landmark. It is now open for guided tours, and contains a gift shop. Jamaicans still believe it is haunted. Tours of the house end early so that all of the employees can leave before Annie's spirit comes out to wander.

Many visitors report strange images appearing in their developed photographs. Some report the appearance of woman's face in the mirror in Annie's bedroom. Others report glowing or foggy areas appearing on the bed in Annie's room and sometimes in other areas of the house. Visitors have also reported that the film they used in certain rooms of the house would not develop, while the rest of the roll was fine. Others say that all the pictures they shot inside to house develop with a misty look, while outdoor photos are clear. Some of these mysterious photographs have been sent to Rose Hall and are displayed in the gift shop.

64. The Busby Stoop

The Busby Stoop Inn at Kirby Wiske a village near Thirsk, takes its odd name from an 18th century owner and his 'stoop' or tall chair. It is the chair that is haunted or rather cursed; the disreputable Busby appears to have eked out his living by coin-clipping. Thieving and receiving stolen goods he was eventually sentenced to death for murder of a female relative. As he was dragged from his inn he swore that anyone who sat in his 'stoop' would die as violently and suddenly as he himself was about to do; Simon Theaskston, whose brewery owned the pub until 1978 said the legend may be odd and vague, but it is a matter of record that in the last 200 years or so death has

struck anyone who dared to sit in the chair within a very short time. They said that many who sat in the chair were dead within days! or even hours. Eventually the chair was moved out of harm's way.

It has to be said that many of the chairs victims of the last few decades could be categorised as 'high risk' anyway. They included an RAF pilot (killed the following day). A motorist (who crashed the next day and died of his injuries), a motocyclist (killed shortly after leaving the pub), a holiday hitch-hiker (knocked down and killed two days later) and a local man in his late thirties (who died of a massive heart attack the following night). But the odds against all of them dying so soon after sitting in the Busby stoop must be high enough to suggest this was no mere coincidence.

65. Barney Duffy's Curse

Barney Duffy was a giant of a man. He towered over the two young soldiers, uttering a terrible curse: "Take me or report me, ye red-coated, lily-livered lice! Aye! And then I'll hang – but hear me curse on ye! So surely as ye do this, before me corpse has hung a week on King's Town gallows, ye'll meet a violent death, the pair of ye!"

Duffy, an Irishman, had been imprisoned by the British on Norfolk Island in the Pacific Ocean, 1450 km north-east of Sydney. The island is one of the most beautiful in the world, but its past is a long tale of blood.

Present day residents have claimed to have seen ghosts of the Bounty mutineers, who outgrew tiny Pitcairn Island and moved to Norfolk in the 19th century.

Barney Duffy escaped from his hell, and hid in a hollow pine in the thick rain forest. He emerged at night to raid the vegetable gardens of the settlement. His beard and hair were long and matted, and he had just a few rags to cover himself when the two soldiers who were out fishing, discovered him.

They ignored his curse, and returned him to the settlement. Duffy was hanged, and two days later the soldiers went to fish near the same pine.

Shortly after a foot patrol found the broken and battered bodies of the two soldiers drifting in the tide.

No one knows how they died. The secret lies in Barney Duffy Gully on Norfolk Island.

66. Restless Coffins

In the churchyard of Christ Church, Barbados, on a headland overlooking Oistin's Bay, stands a small but strongly built stone tomb. It has been empty since 1820, and seems likely to remain so. Designed as a quiet resting place for the dead, it proved to be anything but that.

The family vault, built of large blocks of local coral stone firmly cemented together, is recessed two feet deep into solid limestone rock. The floor space is 12 feet long by 6½ feet wide; originally the entrance was closed by a heavy slab of blue Devon marble, which sealed the tomb between interments. It was built in 1724 by the widow of an English aristocrat, whose body does not seem to have been interred there unless his coffin was subsequently removed. The first recorded interment is that of Mrs. Thomasina Goddard on July 31, 1807.

In the following year the tomb came into the possession of the wealthy Chase family, whose head was Thomas Chase. On February 22, 1808, the small lead coffin of Mary Chase, his infant daughter, was interred in the vault. Four years passed and another Chase daughter, Dorcas, died – of uncertain age but apparently an adult. She was interred in the tomb on July 6, 1812. At that point there was nothing out of the ordinary in the state of the other two coffins.

Matters were very different when, on August 9 the same year, Thomas Chase himself was brought to the tomb. The coffins of both his daughters had been shifted – it looked as though by violence. That of the infant Mary had been thrown across the vault and lay head downward against the far wall.

The black labourers were alarmed at the sight, but the Chase family did not seem unduly upset. The coffins were returned to their original places beside the undisturbed one of Mrs. Goddard, and Thomas Chase's was placed alongside them. His was an exceedingly heavy lead coffin, requiring eight men to lift it. When the marble slab of the vault was put in position, great care was taken to seal it properly.

On the death of Samuel Brewster Ames, a baby who may have been a Chase relative, his coffin was brought to the tomb on September 25, 1816. All the coffins were in confusion, save that of Mrs. Goddard. Her coffin, which had been made of wood, had disintegrated but was in its place; the others had been flung about and upended. Thomas Chase's heavy lead coffin was lying on its side several feet to the left of its original spot. This time the Chase family was furious, assuming that the desecration was linked with the abortive slave rising that had been crushed with much bloodshed earlier in the year. But apart from the unlikelihood that the superstitious blacks would be willing to enter a tomb, the sheer weight of Thomas Chase's coffin made it a well-nigh impossible task to have been accomplished unnoticed.

The coffins were rearranged, and the marble slab cemented into position. On November 17 of the same year, the tomb had to be opened again to receive Samuel Brewster, who had been murdered during the slave uprising and temporarily buried elsewhere. Once again the coffins were in the wildest disorder. Except for Mrs. Goddard's – undisturbed as always – they were leaning against the walls, crossing and overlapping each other. This time the minister of Christ Church, a magistrate, and two other men searched the vault thoroughly. They found no crack, no concealed entrance. A fairly big crowd had accompanied the funeral procession, and the findings confirmed their worst fears: the Chase Tomb was cursed. The black labourers had to be ordered sharply to enter the tomb and restore order. Mrs. Goddard's bones, which had fallen out of her disintegrating coffin, were wrapped up and placed against the wall. Once again the entrance was sealed.

Three years passed before the next, and last, coffin was brought to the Chase Tomb. The tomb's troubled history had created such sensational interest in Barbados that the governor, Lord Combermere, the commander of the garrison, and many hundreds of spectators walked behind the coffin of Mrs. Thomasina Clarke on July 17, 1819. The vault was opened only with difficulty because Thomas Chase's heavy coffin was upended and resting against it, six feet from the place it should have been. The two children's coffins, which had rested on top of two larger ones, were on the floor. Only Mrs. Goddard's, the flimsiest of them all, was untouched.

Lord Combermere had been one of the Duke of Wellington's most successful cavalry commanders against Napoleon. It took a lot to frighten him. He personally supervised a meticulous examination of the interior of the vault. When nothing had been revealed by this search, he had the seven coffins put back into position, and ordered fine white beach sand to be sprinkled on the floor. This would show the footprints of anyone who entered the vault. The marble slab was put in place, and Lord Combermere and several others imprinted their personal seals in the wet cement sealing the slab.

Nine months later, on April 19, 1820, Lord Combermere was in the neighbourhood of Christ Church again. He was due to return to England that year and was curious to know whether anything had happened inside the Chase Tomb. He found the seals on the slab unbroken. No footprints appeared on the sanded floor. The remains of Mrs. Goddard's coffin were against the wall where they had been left. But again the other coffins had been flung all over the place. One child's coffin was lying just inside the entrance. Thomas Chase's particularly heavy coffin and another one were upside down.

Experienced campaigner as he was, Lord Combermere knew when a situation was beyond his control. He ordered the coffins to be removed and buried elsewhere. Since then, the tomb had remained empty.

What power disturbed the coffins has never been discovered. Barbados suffers from earthquakes, but no quake would overturn a lead coffin and leave fragile wood unmoved. No moisture was ever detected in the vault, but even if water had somehow entered it and been able to shift the coffins, the wooden one would have been the first to move – and yet its position remained unaltered. Neither of these natural explanations – which seem to be the only two – are convincing. It also seems impossible that a human agency was involved. What about the supernatural?

Thomas Chase was the most hated man on the island. Both he and his daughter Dorcas were believed to have killed themselves – she, it was said, starved herself to death out of despair over her cruel father. The disorders began after her interment, as though the other corpses resented the presence of a suicide among them. Could some power associated with the corpse of Mrs. Goddard – whose coffin always remained undisturbed – have flung the coffins about the vault? Could the arrival of a second suicide and the corpses of three who did not die by their own hand have intensified the power? If the answer to these questions is "yes," the mystery still remains of what that power is, and why it manifested itself in this particular case. The curse on the Chase Tomb is as much a puzzle today as when it confronted the citizens of Barbados in the 19th century.

67. Lemp Mansion

Lemp Mansion is believed to be one of the most haunted places in St. Louis City, and in the top 10 of most haunted in North America, located at 3322 De Menil Pl., across Highway 55, across from the Anheuser-Busch Brewery in the Soulard Area.

The Lemp Family seemed to be cursed with death and depression.

It is believed the curse of the Lemp Family started with

William Lemp Sr.'s son, Frederick Lemp. Frederick's death, believed to have been a heart attack from being over worked, caused William Sr. to fall into a deep depression, leading to him committing suicide in his bedroom by shooting himself, and killing his dog.

The next to commit suicide was Frederick's sister, Elsa. Though not in the Lemp Mansion when she killed herself, her home is believed to be haunted as well.

William Jr. later married Lillian Hadlan. She was a beautiful young woman.

Her favourite colour was lavender and that is all she wore, thus her being nicknamed "The Lavender Lady". They eventually divorce causing a great scandal all of St. Louis would talk about, causing Lillian to go into seclusion.

There is a rumour that there was a child born around this time (possibly from an affair William Jr. had with a servant) supposedly this child was mentally retarded, and deformed in some way, causing the family to keep him a secret to avoid humiliation or disgrace. They only know the child by the name of Monkey Boy. There is no record of a child like this being born to the Lemp's, but he has let himself to be known by psychics that have toured the home.

William Jr. eventually joined the rest of his family by shooting himself in the chest with a revolver, in the office on the first floor of Lemp Mansion, now a dining room!

In the 1970s the mansion was sold to Dick Pointer who started renovations on the mansion. Many of the workers started complaining of being watched by unseen, unwelcoming eyes, disappearing tools, apparitions of a gentleman in black, and eerie, unexplained sounds.

Many of these workers left never to return to the site.

Now Lemp Mansion is a bed and breakfast where many employees and guests report sightings of the Lavender Lady, a phantom dog barking, cold spots, the feelings of being watched, disembodied voices, even glasses being picked up from off the bar by unseen hands.

Anyone is welcomed to decide for themselves. The next time you're in St. Louis, maybe you might want to check out Lemp Mansion. You can even reserve the room that William Lemp Sr. killed himself in!

68. House of Horror

Innkeeper Lazio Kronberg and his wife Susi faced a bleak future in the little Hungarian town of Tisakurt. It was 1919 and the couple had spent their savings trying to keep the inn going throughout the Great War. Now they had hardly enough to buy food.

There were other tragedies. Their only daughter had run away to Budapest, where she was said to be a prostitute. Their eldest son Nicholas had also run away, fleeing the house at the age of nine after Lazio whipped him for failing at school. Their other two sons had died in the war.

Night after night the old couple would sit and discuss the hopeless years ahead. At last they came to the grim decision that there was only one hope – murder for profit.

Carefully, they prepared for the killings. Lazio dug a long trench six feet deep in the woods. He filled it with quicklime, prepared to tell anyone who asked that he was planning to build new out-houses. From the village store Susi brought home a small brown sack filled with strychnine crystals. She told the storekeeper they were going to use it to poison wolves.

Between 1919 and 1912, ten people breathed their last in the Kronberg inn. In all cases, there had been good wine with dinner and an even more remarkable vintage afterwards......heavily laced with strychnine. The couple grew more cautious as their stolen wealth increased. There must be only one more victim, and then the quicklime pit would be sealed forever.

He came on August 14, 1922; a genial fat man in his mid-thirties, with a suitcase so heavy that it must surely contain gold coins. He had been a salesman for years, and was now looking for good land in which to invest his money.

When Susi cooked the evening meal and Lazio served it, the visitor insisted that they must be his guests for supper. And they must call him by his nickname Lucky.

Throughout the festive two-hour meal, the guest talked about his travels and was so friendly that the Kronbergs were reluctant to kill him. But it had to be done, and at last Susi brought in the "special" wine.

Their fat guest died as he drained his glass, convulsing, his lips curled back from his teeth in the final spasm of strychnine poisoning.

In Lucky's bedroom, they searched his bag and saw at once they had been right. There was fortune in gold coins. His hands shaking, Lazio pawed through the dead man's clothes and then saw something else – a snapshot of the Kronbergs themselves!

The couple looked at each other with dawning horror and grief. They had murdered their long-lost son. They left the gold and went back to the dining-room, where Nicholas was slouched at the table. They wrote a short confession and then sat down with him.

Three days later, the villagers found them, all dead from strychnine poisoning.

During the years that followed, few ventured inside the house. Those daring to stay two or three nights with a view to buying the place were always frightened off by the same grisly apparition: the sight of 13 ghostly figures from the 1920s, seated around the dining table. Each had its lips peeled back in a ghastly strychnine grin.

Another World War came and went, the house became dilapidated, but still no one would spend a night inside or even near it. Then on September 23, 1980, flames licking at the evening sky told the village that an arsonist had been at work. The old inn was reduced to ashes. No one tried to find the culprit. No one cared.

Tisakurt was at last free of its house of horror.

69. Skyway To Doom

Has the ghost of an American construction worker put a curse on the Sunshine Skyway Bridge? That was the theory put forward by a Florida fisherman after nearly 60 people died in four separate shipping disasters at the Tampa Bay bridge during the first five months of 1980.

In January, 23 coastguards were killed when their cutter collided with an oil tanker. The following month, a freighter smashed into one of the main bridge supports, and ten days later a tanker ran out of control, and slammed into the main span.

But the worst accident to hit the jinxed bridge came on May 9. Possibly blinded by the wind-lashed rain of a violent storm, the skipper of a 10,000-ton Liberian Freighter, *Summit Venture*, misjudged his approach to the bridge. Instead of passing under the middle of it, the ship ploughed into one of the main supports, and a huge section of the road running over it collapsed.

Cars, trucks and a Greyhound bus plunged 150 feet into the water; 32 people died, 23 of them on the bus. Other drivers missed death by inches, slamming on their brakes just in time as the yawning gap opened up in front of them.

The Florida House of Representatives stood for a moment's silence as news of the tragedy reached them during a meeting. One member blamed the Tampa Bay harbour pilot system, and called for an inquiry.

But a local fisherman, 27-year-old Charlie Williams, said later: "When the bridge was being built, a construction worker fell into some wet concrete. He's still there, in the structure. The Skyway has been cursed ever since."

The bridge, which is four miles long, was opened in September 1954. More than 40 people have committed suicide by leaping from it.

70. Suicide Song

In 1935 Lazzlo Javor, a Hungarian poet, wrote a song called *Gloomy Sunday*. This was later put to music by Rezsoe Seres and the record became a hit.

Lazzlo Javor's former girl-friend, for whom the song had been written, committed suicide shortly after the record's release. Her suicide note said, *Gloomy Sunday*. A short while later a Hungarian government official shot himself. He was found slumped over a copy of lyrics of *Gloomy Sunday*. Next, a girl tried to poison herself. When she was found, *Gloomy Sunday* was still playing on the gramophone in the room. In a Budapest restaurant a young man shot himself – the band had just played *Gloomy Sunday*.

The Hungarian government banned all public performances of the song, for the situation was fast getting out of hand. In Britain, where other suicides had been reported, the BBC banned the song. Similar suicides were reported in America but the government decided not to ban it in the USA.

In all, there were some 200 suicides around the world that were said to be connected with *Gloomy Sunday*. In 1968, a Hungarian jumped to his death from the eighth floor of a building. It was Rezsoe Seres, who had never been able to write another hit after *Gloomy Sunday*!

References

1. Rupert Matthews – The Super Chilling Book of Horror, 1988.
2. Nigel Blunder & Roger Boar – The World's Greatest Ghosts, 1983.
3. Ripleys – Belive It or Not. Vol. 5, 1958.
4. Colin Wilson – The Encyclopaedia of Ghosts, 1985.
5. Robert Heinl – Written in Blood.
6. Antony Hippisley Coxe – Haunted Britain, 1974.
7. Peters Eldin – Amazing Ghosts and Ghouls, 1987.
8. Warren Smith – Strange Women of the Occult, 1968.
9. Charles Berlitz – World of Strange Phenomena. Vol. I & II, 1989.
10. Peter Haining – Ghosts, Illustrated History, 1974.
11. Uday Lal – Book of Mysterious Events.
12. Daniel Cohen – Ghost in the House, 1995.
13. Ripley – Creepy Stuff, 2001.
14. Colin Wilson – Enigmas and Mysteries, 1976.
15. The Reader's Digest – Mysteries of the Unknown, 1985.
16. Peter Underwood – Haunted London.

17. Fortean Times – No. 34, Winter 1981, - p-16.
18. The Unexplained – Mysteries of Mind Space and Time, Vol. 13.
19. D. Scott Rogo – The Poltergeist Experience, pp. 261-268.
20. Vincent Gaddis – Invisible Horizons.
21. Jeremy Kingston – Mysterious Happening, 1991.
22. Vikas Khatri – True Ghosts & Spooky Incidents, 2006.
23. Uday Lal – ABC of Mysteries, 1992.
24. F.S. Edsall – The World of Psychic Phenomena, Pp. 12-13.
25. Frank Smyth – Ghosts and Poltergeists, p.60.
26. William G. Roll – The Poltergeist, p.38.
27. Charles Fort – The Complete Books of Charles Fort, pp. 577-81.
28. Andrew Mac Kenzie – A Gallery of Ghosts, pp. 139-41.
29. Colin Wilson – Mysteries, 1978.
30. Colin Wilson – Strange but True, 1994.
31. The Reader's Digest, Eds., Mysteries of the Unexplained, 1985.
32. Charles G. Harper – Haunted Houses, pp. 116-20.
33. Robert Dale Owen – Footfalls on the Boundary of Another World, pp. 333-40.
34. Raymond Lamont Brown – Phantom Soldiers, pp. 80-81.
35. American Anthropologist, New Series 44:169-70, April-June 1942.

36. American Anthropologist, New Series 44:170-71, April-June 1942.
37. Science Digest, 80:45, August 1976.
38. The Reader's Digest, Eds., Folklore, Myths, and Legends of Britain, pp. 106-107.
39. Mary Bolte – Haunted New England : A Devilish Views of the Yankee Past, pp. 43-46.
40. John Goddwin – Unsolved: The World of the Unknown.
41. Ronald Rose – Living Magic.
42. Edmund Gurney et al – Phantasms of the Living, pp. 493-94.
43. Philip Van Doren Stern – The Breathless Moments.
44. Mathew Manning – Poltergeist.
45. Several Issues of Fortean Times
46. Psychosomatic Medicine, 26:104-107. 1964.
47. Gyles Brandreth – 1000 Horrors, The Most Horrific Book Ever Known, 1983.
48. Jenny Randles – Paranormal Source Book, 1999.
49. Mike Dash – Borderlands, 1997.
50. Ian Wilson – Life After Death, 1997.
51. Hilary Evans – Visions, Apparitions, Alien Entities, 1984.
52. Warren Beath – The Death of James Dean.
53. Loren Coleman – Curious Encounters, 1986.
54. Celia Green and Charles Mc Crecry – Apparitions, 1975.
55. Richard Davis – The Encyclopaedia of Horrors, 1987.
56. Nigel Blundell – Facts or Fiction, The Supernatural, 1996.

57. John Guy – Ghosts, Haunted Houses and Spooky Stories, 1999.
58. Lethbridge, T.C. et al – Ghosts and Ghouls, 1961.
59. Brooks, J.A – Ghosts and Legends of the Lake District, 1988.
60. John Spencer and Tony Wells – Ghost Watching, 1994.
61. Colin Wilson – Poltergeist, 1993.
62. Thomas Allen – Possessed, 1993.
63. Thurston Hopkins – Adventures with Phantoms, 1958.
64. Elliot O' Donnell – Twenty Years Experiences as Ghost Hunter, 1996.
65. Daniel Cohen – The Phantom Hitchhiker, 1995.
66. John and Anne Spencer – Encyclopaedia of Ghosts and Spirits, 1992.
67. Christina Hole – Haunted England, 1990.
68. Paul Hamlyn – Larousse Encyclopaedia of Mythology, 1959.
69. Time Life – Phantom Encounters, 1987.
70. The Readers Digest's Book of Strange Stories, Amazing Facts, 1975.
71. Guy Lyon Playfair – This House is Haunted, 1980.

by the same author

60/-

Pages: 128

80/-

Pages: 160

80/-

Pages: 152

80/-

Pages: 176

80/-

Pages: 136

80/-

Pages: 112

Postage: Rs. 15/- on each book.

Every subsequent book: Rs. 5/- extra.